CRYPTOCURRENCIES

Learn How to Use the Next Generation of the Financial System to Win

by Dejan "Deki" Markovic

Cryptocurrencies: Learn How to Use the Next Generation of the Financial System to Win

www.CryptocurrenciesBook.com

Copyright © 2018 Dejan Marković

ISBN-13: 978-1-77277-206-7

Limits of Liability and Disclaimer of Warranty

The author and publisher shall not be liable for your misuse of the enclosed material. This book is strictly for informational and educational purposes only. The purpose of this book is to educate and entertain. The author and/or publisher do not guarantee that anyone following these techniques, suggestions, tips, ideas, or strategies will become successful. The author and/or publisher shall have neither liability nor responsibility to anyone with respect to any loss or damage caused, or alleged to be caused, directly or indirectly by the information contained in this book.

Legal / Financial / Investment Disclaimer

This book and the accompanying website are for information and illustrative purposes only and do not purport to show actual results. It is not and should not be regarded as investment advice or as a recommendation regarding any particular security or course of action. Opinions expressed herein are only current opinions of the author, as of the date appearing in this material only and are subject to change without notice. The data is for illustrational purposes only and the information provided within this book changes rapidly and some data can be out dated.

Publisher: 10-10-10 Publishing, Canada
First Edition March 2018
Second Edition April 2018

Printed in the United States of America and Slovenia

| Table of Contents |

| Acknowledgments |

There are many people in my life who I should thank. I became who I am because of them. Here is a short list of acknowledgments. Anyone who has been left out will be thanked when we meet again.

To my wife **Jelka Holz** who gave me endless support for success in business and this book. Without her I would probably still be a regular trumpet player - someone from the crowd. I love you so much!

To my eight and five-year-old daughters for inspiration and love of life. They are bringing me happiness and joy.

To my parents, brother and brother-in-law, especially to my mother who is constantly supporting me with delicious lunches, great help with the kids, encouragement and a place where I can rest. I also thank my parents-in-law for help and believing in me.

To Robert Rolih, for all the knowledge and wisdom about entrepreneurship, marketing and investments that you shared with me. You are a perfect example.

To John Barksdale for inspiring me with his visions, techniques, achievements and for the possibility of cooperation.

To my crypto IT friends for helping me understand the crypto world and giving me knowledge, so now I can help others.

To my respectable friend Rodney Loo for sharing advice and wisdom with me. I deeply respect you.

To my good friend, Jarle, who inspires and supports me in business and who brought me to another level.

To my friend and business partner, Nigel, who showed me how to become a very good leader and stage speaker.

To my long-time friend Franci "Frenk" for introducing and firing me up for the crypto world.

To my dear friend Gabor for help, collaboration, hospitality and long-time friendship.

To my friend and business partner, Urban, who taught me about leadership and helped me endlessly in the most difficult period of my life.

To Mitja, "Mičo," my brother from another mother, who also stood with me in the most desperate period of my life. I love you brother!

To my friend and business partner, Frank, for hospitality and for giving me a big push in developing my business.

To my soul friends, Primož and Barbara, who are teaching me and my wife how beautiful life can be and who share their wisdom as to how to create a wonderful relationship.

To a big group of friends and supporters from all over the world: Srečko, Primož, Janko, Tone, Narcis, Milan, Jure, Roman, Simon, Ivana, Igor "Schmittah," Boris "BB," Vojko "Vojc," Tomaž, Marjan, Matjaž, Edita, Andrej, Peter, Zdravko, Boris, Darko, Iviliana, Denis, Mitja, Alen, Martin, Oto, Tina, Živan, Iztok, Dušan, Mojca, Igor, Kristjan, Francisco, Vasco, Jose, Pedro, Ivan, Alex, Santi, Hicham, Nadia, Romano, Carlo, Alex, Vadim, Matei, Viktor, Sandor, Vlad, Michael, Stijn, Tomasz, Slavko, Nina, Ewald and many many others.

To Clayton Bye for all his support and advice in realising this book.

To my clients and supporters who helped me become better in my business and personal development.

To Randy Gage for sharing his wisdom on Prosperity TV. Through it I have learned that we all deserve prosperity and abundance and that I deserve it too. I became a better person because of him!

To people who influenced my life through education:
Paul O'Mahony, Kevin Green, Aleksander Šinigoj, Jessen James Chinnapan, Tom "Big Al" Schreiter and many more.

The very special thanks to Loral Langemeier for accompanying this book with her powerful vision and enhancing energy.

And super special thanks to Raymond Aaron who encouraged me to write this book. Also, thanks to Raymond's team who supported me in making this book happen.

| Foreword |

Dejan Deki Markovic, who is a successful entrepreneur and award-winning author, has chosen to share with you one of the hottest topics in today's financial world.

The topic? Cryptocurrency, something many people feel is poised to be the next chapter in the development of the world's financial system. The author mostly focuses on BitCoin, which was the first cryptocurrency to appear on the net.

He will show you what cryptocurrency is, how it started, what you can do with it and why it is being seen by some as *The Next Generation of the Financial System.* Dejan is an expert in the world of cryptocurrency and will share his secrets with you. If that's not enough, he's also available as an advisor, coach or mentor. **Contact Dejan at cryptocurrenciesbook@gmail.com**

This fantastic book will capture your imagination from the first Chapter, *The Birth of Cryptocurrency,* through to the last word in Chapter 18, which is about how to choose and use both *Paper and Offline Wallets.* From mining the internet for brand new cryptocoins to investing in existing coins to using the currency at a retail level, Dejan will walk you through the fascinating world of decentralized banking. No more government interference or oversight; this is the wild west all over again—cryptocurrency's value is usually based on the popularity of the specific brand of coin (and there are many) rather than gold, silver or some other real material world value.

Did you know you can have your own cryptocurrency to be used in your own economy? How exciting is that? And as an investment? Fortunes are being made. Capital ventures have been undertaken by such companies as NASDAQ, BANK OF AMERICA, MERRIL LYNCH, ING GROUP and even WELLS FARGO, to name a few.

The bottom line is that the book, **Cryptocurrencies,** offers up everything you could ever want to know about cryptocurrency. It's a journey from the very beginning of the mystery shrouded BitCoin, through its development to a legitimate form of international currency and beyond. Both the good and bad, the pros and the cons and even an example of real-life use are included in this brilliant book.

I highly recommend it …

Loral Langemeier—*Millionaire Maker*
Loral Langemeier is a money expert, sought after speaker, entrepreneurial thought leader, and best-selling author of five books who is on a relentless mission to change the conversation about money and empower people around the world to become millionaires.

| Introduction |

People are constantly coming to me and asking to be taught about cryptocurrencies. They want to know what is going on in this field, and what the scenes are behind the cryptocurrency world.

A few years ago, I was like you. I didn't know anything about cryptocurrencies. All I had was a bunch of questions and the feeling that this was something I didn't want to miss. My intuition told me that this new form of money was the future, and I wanted to be part of it. I found professionals, and I learned from them. I also did my own research, eventually partnering with IT people who really understood what was going on—offering various products and services connected to the crypto world. This industry is really starting to open up, and there has never been a better time to get involved. This book is meant to help you do just that.

A friend of mine invests in real estate and also works as a day trader. I recently asked him if he had considered investing in cryptocurrencies.

He said, "No. I don't know anything about them. I wouldn't feel comfortable doing that."
I told him that I was writing a book about cryptocurrencies and asked him if he would like a copy when I was done.
He replied, "Sure! I would really be interested in learning about this."

I have so many examples where people are excited about what they are seeing happen in the crypto world, but at the same time, they really don't understand enough to get involved. This book will give you everything you need to know to take that step forward—in simple terms that anyone will be able to understand.

My friend, a professional writer, mentioned that the more he learns about this field, the more excited he becomes. He is actively looking for ways to invest in cryptocurrencies and wants to actually use this type of money in the retail world.

There are many people in similar situations: people who want to make the leap to cryptocurrencies but just don't have the knowledge to do so. This book will solve their problem. It will open a door to the crypto world.

People often face challenges or issues sending money from one part of the world to another (between Europe, Asia, America, Australia, etc.). Sending a cryptocurrency is a fast and cheap (low fees) solution …

Cryptocurrency is a serious thing. As of 2016, there were more than 70 million places where you could use bitcoins. There are cash machines and gas stations where you can buy bitcoins for daily use. Many retail outlets exist that accept cryptocurrency bitcoins as payment. This includes brick-and-mortar businesses like restaurants, apartments, and law firms, as well as popular online services such as Namecheap, Overstock.com, and Reddit. By the end of April 2017, the total value of all existing bitcoins exceeded 20 billion US dollars, with millions of dollars' worth of bitcoins exchanged daily. The opportunities for use (and for investing) are endless.

Yet … it's like cryptocurrency is a public secret. The book, CRYPTOCURRENCIES, will reveal this secret to you.

| Encouragement |

By reading this book, there exists a high probability that you'll find words that might be new to you; but be brave. At the end of the book, there's a glossary with explanations. I also encourage you to use the Internet, where you can find many descriptions or explanations— just Google it.

Life is like a river, always bringing new challenges and updates. The crypto world is the same. So, the newest details and updates regarding this fascinating industry can also be searched on the internet.

And also, I am there for you—available for courses/seminars, etc.

You can connect with Deki at **cryptocurrenciesbook@gmail.com**

CHAPTER 1
THE BIRTH OF CRYPTOCURRENCY

| **Chapter 1** - The Birth of Cryptocurrency |

In ancient days, essential commodities were used as money (grain, oil, wine and animals are good examples). Coins slowly made their way into society and, in what is now Europe, the Knights Templar (having a need for safekeeping the money of the travelers they protected) created the first banking system. With the further modernization of society, the need to track money and value across large territories of land resulted in the birth of paper and coin money, issued from ruling governments. Then came the advent of credit and debit cards—electronic substitutes for physical currencies. This was followed, about a quarter of a century ago, by an invention called the world wide web, which made it possible for people to buy and sell virtually anything to anyone around the world, using bank-issued credit cards or money-changing companies like PayPal. Finally, just a few years ago, a new form of money native to the Internet was born: cryptocurrency. In this book, we explore what this new type of money is, how it works, and how you can get involved in what amounts to a digital revolution.

Cryptocurrency is a digital currency that's created and managed through the use of advanced encryption techniques known as cryptography. Instead of relying on a centralized company (a bank) to govern the economic system, cryptography allows the entire network to exist publicly, without triggering privacy concerns. In other words, cryptocurrency is an OPEN SYSTEM that allows for the independent creation and distribution of digital assets (money, coins, tokens, etc.).

Cryptocurrency went from being a concept to reality with the creation of Bitcoin in 2008/2009, by an unknown independent or group of people called Satoshi Nakamoto. Bitcoin garnered a growing following in subsequent years, but it didn't grab investor and media attention until April 2013, when it peaked at a record $266 per bitcoin (30th November 2013, highest peak was $1149.14, cap was $13.85B). Bitcoin captured a market value of over $2 billion at that first peak, but a 50% plunge shortly afterward sparked a raging debate about the future of cryptocurrencies in general and Bitcoin in particular.

So, will these alternative currencies eventually supplant conventional currencies and become as common as dollars and euros? Or are cryptocurrencies a passing fad? I believe the answer lies with Bitcoin and the entire crypto world.

| Notes |

CHAPTER 2
BITCOIN—
THE CURRENT
STANDARD

_____

| **Chapter 2 -** Bitcoin—the Current Standard |

In simple terms, Bitcoin is a currency that isn't issued or guaranteed by any bank. Instead, some time ago, everyday people, like you and me, used their (powerful) computers to mine the digital money. Today, only the most organized, big mining facilities mine Bitcoin. Anyway, the mining process involves such things as the solving of complex algorithms and the verifying of Bitcoin transactions. You're rewarded for the use of your computer with bitcoins. These coins are currently being issued at the rate of 12.5 bitcoins every 10 minutes (starting with 50 BTC and 25 BTC per block before the first and second halving). They'll be capped at 21 million, a level that's expected to be reached in 2140. Thus, like the mining of gold, bitcoins will become scarcer as time goes on. It also follows that this type of mining will be more labor intensive as the years pass by.

Bitcoins are fundamentally different from regular or fiat currency.

1. Fiat currency is backed by the full faith and credit of the issuing government. Bitcoins are not issued by any bank and are truly international in nature.

2. Fiat currency issuance is a highly centralized activity, supervised by a nation's central bank. While the bank regulates the amount of money issued, there is really no upper limit to the amount of such currency issuance. In fact, there have been times in history when people have had to take baskets of money with them to do their daily shopping, so devalued had become the currency. This happened because the government(s) had kept printing money when there were no valuables (like gold, silver, diamonds, etc.) to back that currency. Bitcoin is a decentralized, unregulated, open book type of currency. Much of the Bitcoin mining activities revolve around verifying that all Bitcoin transactions are real and recorded. In addition, there will never be more than 21 million bitcoins in existence.

3. Local currency deposits are generally insured against bank failures by a government body. Bitcoin, on the other hand, has no support mechanisms. The value of a bitcoin is dependent on what investors are willing to pay for it at a given point in time. As well, if a bitcoin exchange folds up, clients with Bitcoin balances have no recourse to get them back. Keep in mind that there were times in history when banks collapsed; for example, The Barings Bank case, where money lost value almost overnight.

| Why Bitcoin? |

It's cheap

Let's compare Bitcoin to credit/debit card transactions, which are instantaneous, too. Merchants pay for the privilege of using credit cards or a debit cards. Some of them will, in turn, charge a fee for debit card transactions. Bitcoin transaction fees are minimal or, in some cases, free. An example of this is inside some systems when transactions stay on the same BTC address, so they don't burden the blockchain.

The central government can't take your cryptocurrencies away. Do you remember what happened in Cyprus, during March 2013? The Central Bank wanted to take back uninsured deposits larger than $100,000, to help recapitalize itself. This caused major unrest. It also wanted to take a percentage of deposits below that figure, eating directly into family savings. That can't happen with Bitcoin because the currency is decentralized; you own it. No central authority has control, so a bank can't take your Bitcoins away from you. If you are like me and have found your trust in the traditional banking system unraveling, that's a big benefit.

There are no chargebacks

Once bitcoins have been sent, they're gone. A person who has sent bitcoins can't retrieve them without the recipient's consent. This makes it difficult to commit the kind of fraud that we often see with credit cards, where people make a purchase, collect the product, and then ask the credit card company for a chargeback.

People can't steal your payment information from merchants

This is important. When credit cards appeared, the Internet hadn't yet been conceived. It follows that credit cards were never supposed to be used online. In fact, webforms insist that you must enter your secret information (credit card number, expiry date, and CSV number). Can you think of a less secure way to do online business? It's why credit card numbers keep being stolen.

On the other hand, Bitcoin transactions don't ask you to give up any secret information. None! Instead, they use two keys: one public and one private. Anyone can see the public key (it's your bitcoin address), but your private key is secret. Whenever you send a bitcoin, you just sign the transaction by using both keys and apply a certain mathematical function to them. This creates what is called a certificate, which proves the transaction came from you. As long as you don't do anything illogical, like publishing your private key, you'll be safe.

It isn't inflationary

The problem with regular (fiat) currency is that governments can print as much of it as they like, something they frequently do. If there aren't enough US dollars to pay off the national debt, then the Federal Reserve can simply print more. If the economy is floundering, then the government can create money and inject it—very publicly—through a process called quantitative easing, which causes the value of the currency to decrease.

Look at it this way: If you double the number of dollars in circulation, there are suddenly two dollars where before there was just one. Someone who was selling a chocolate bar for a dollar will now have to double the price if it's to retain the same value as before. Why? Because the dollar has only half its value. This increase in the price of goods and services is called inflation. And it follows that inflation will tend to decrease people's buying power. How does Bitcoin avoid inflation? It was designed to have a maximum number of coins. Only 21 million Bitcoins can ever be created (under the original specification). This eliminates the possibility of inflation. In fact, deflation—where the price of goods and services falls—is more probable in the Bitcoin world.

It's as private as you want it to be

Don't want people to know what you've purchased? Bitcoin can provide this kind of privacy while also offering transaction transparency. Thanks to the "blockchain" everyone knows how many transactions a given bitcoin address holds. They can also see where those transactions come from, and where they've been sent. But, unlike conventional bank accounts, nobody knows who's holding a particular Bitcoin address. It's like having found a clear plastic wallet. Everyone can see inside it, but no one knows who it belongs to. However, I believe it's worth mentioning that people who always use the same Bitcoin address or who combine coins from multiple addresses into a single address risk making it easier to identify them online.

You don't need to trust anyone else

In a conventional banking system, you must trust people to handle your money properly. For example, you have to trust the bank employees, third-party payment processors and even the merchants you deal with. These organizations also demand important, sensitive pieces of information from you. But as Bitcoin is decentralized, you don't need to trust anyone when using it. A transaction is digitally signed and secure. An anonymous miner will verify it, and then the transaction is completed. The merchant need not even know who you are.

You own it

There's no other electronic cash system where your account isn't owned by someone else. PayPal, for example, can decide that your account has been misused. In this instance, it has the power to freeze all of your assets held in the account--without consulting you. You must then jump through whatever hoops they deem are necessary to get it cleared. With Bitcoin, you own the two keys that make up a Bitcoin address. Nobody can take the keys away from you (unless you lose them yourself, or you host your account with a web-based wallet service that then loses them for you).

You can create your own money

National governments everywhere take a dim view of you producing your own money. With Bitcoin, however, it's encouraged. You can buy bitcoins on the open market, or you can also mine your own coins, provided you have enough computing power. Once you've covered your initial investment (in equipment and electricity), mining bitcoins is just a case of leaving the computer on and the software running. Who wouldn't like their computer to earn them money while they sleep?

| Notes |

| Notes |

CHAPTER 3
THE BIG GUYS

| **Chapter 3 -** The Big Guys |

Who are they, why are they investing, how much are they investing, and why is no one speaking publicly about it? This is a serious matter, and it is important for all the people. After all, cryptocurrency is poised to become the next financial market. Take a look at the information chart below—you may be surprised at what you find.

Allow me to ask you this: Why do you think these large companies have taken a position in the cryptocurrency market—especially when the system has been publicly resisting Bitcoin, but at the same time, they were investing in cryptocurrency? R3 has invested 107 million USD in Bitcoin infrastructure. R3 is a group of investors, including Bank of America, Merrill Lynch, HSBC, Intel, SBI Group, Temasek Holdings, Banco Bradesco, Barclays PLC, ING Group, Itau Unibanco, Natixis, UBC, and Wells Fargo.

Company	R3	Stratumn	POSaBIT	OB1
Date	23-May-2017	8-Jun-2017	29-Jun-2017	2-Jun-2017
Cumulative Funding $	107,000,000	7,670,000	1,500,000	4,200,000
Round Size $	107,000,000	7,000,000	1,500,000	200,000
Classification	Infrastructure	Financial Services	Payment processor	Financial Services
Investors	Bank of America Merrill Lynch, HSBC, Intel, SBI Group, Temasek Holdings, Banco Bradesco, Barclays PLC, ING Group, Itau Unibanco, Natixis, UBC, Wells Fargo	Open CNP, NASDAQ, Otium Capital, Digital Currency Group	Digital Currency Group	Digital Currency Group
Round	Series A	Series A	Seed	Venture
Country	United States	France	United States	United States
Region	US & Canada	Europe	US & Canada	US & Canada
Headquarter	New York	Paris	Seattle	Washington DC

| Notes |

CHAPTER 4
THE CRYPTO WORLD

| **Chapter 4 -** The Crypto World |

At today's market opening (July 10, 2017), the global value of Bitcoin was $2,507.25 USD. So, you can see that it has made great headway since 2013. How has it fared in the eye of the public, over the last four years? Here are some statistics I found on the Internet …

CoinDesk Research recently tapped into the community to gain more intimate insights into the perception and sentiment around Bitcoin, and the second runner, Ethereum. They received more than 1,100 responses. What follows is a sample of the comments received:

- At one point, Bitcoin averaged 287,000 transactions per day, at fees averaging $0.62 each, leading 67% of the surveyed community to say they feel bad about the current state of transaction fees and confirmation times.

- More people now view Bitcoin as digital gold rather than digital currency, and 86% of the community believes Ethereum is just as good.

- 47% think we'll see a contentious hard fork of Bitcoin. But rather than preferring SegWit, or a block-size increase, more individuals believe some combination of solutions is the best short-term scaling solution (For a discussion of Segwit, see the chapter on Blockchain).

- The majority of the community believes we'll see the Lightning Network (see below) used on Bitcoin, and both Raiden and Proof-of-Stake used on Ethereum, in 2018.

- Almost 50% of people are either negative or positive regarding Bitcoin, while less than 5% of people have responded negatively to the Ethereum.

- Despite Hyperledger's (see below) multiple open-source frameworks, live proof of concepts, 130- plus member list, and backing by the Linux Foundation, 87% of people have slight to no knowledge of the group.

- Enterprise Ethereum Alliance, launching in February, was seen as the primary price driver of Ether in Q1.

The Lightning Network is a peer-to-peer (P2P) network that builds upon another network, like Bitcoin or Litecoin, to provide a mesh network of bidirectional payment channels. This currently relies on Segwit.

The payment channels allow participants to transfer money to each other without having to make all their transactions public on the blockchain. This is done by punishing uncooperative participants. When opening a channel, participants must commit an amount (in a funding transaction, which is on the blockchain). Time-based script extensions like CheckSequenceVerify and CheckLockTimeVerify, make the punishment possible.

If we presume a large network of channels on the Bitcoin blockchain, and every Bitcoin user is participating by having at least one channel open on the Bitcoin blockchain, then it's possible to create a near-infinite number of transactions inside this network. The only transactions that are broadcast on the Bitcoin blockchain prematurely are with uncooperative channel counterparties. You should know Ethereum operates differently and is actually using Segwit, where Bitcoin is not.

Vitalik Buterin, the father of Etherium

Hyperledger is an open-source collaborative effort that advances cross-industry blockchain technologies. It's a global collaboration, hosted by The Linux Foundation, including leaders in finance, banking, Internet of Things, supply chains, manufacturing, and technology.

Not since the advent of the Web itself has a technology promised a broader and more fundamental revolution than has blockchain technology. A blockchain is a peer-to-peer distributed ledger that has been forged by consensus and combined with a system for smart contracts and other assistive technologies. Together, these constructions can be used to build a new generation of transactional applications that establish trust, accountability, and transparency at their core, while streamlining business processes and legal constraints.

It's an operating system for marketplaces, data-sharing networks, micro-currencies and decentralized digital communities, one that can markedly reduce the cost and complexity of getting things done in the real world.

Only an open-source, collaborative software development approach can ensure the transparency, longevity, interoperability, and support required to bring blockchain technologies forward to mainstream commercial adoption. That is what Hyperledger is about—communities of software developers building blockchain frameworks and platforms.

| Notes |

| Notes |

CHAPTER 5
ALTERNATIVES
TO BITCOIN

| **Chapter 5** - Alternatives to Bitcoin |

There are different kinds of coins in the crypto world: Bitcoin, Altcoins (Alternative coins), Ethereum, Ethereum-based tokens, and others.

Litecoin - Litecoin came out after Bitcoin, and is designed for processing smaller transactions, faster. It was founded in October 2011, as "a coin that is silver to Bitcoin's gold," according to founder, Charles Lee. Litecoin's maximum limit is 84 million—four times Bitcoin's 21-million limit—and has a transaction processing time of approximately 2.5 minutes, about 1/4 that of Bitcoin.

Ripple - Ripple is a cryptocurrency by OpenCoin, a company that was founded by entrepreneur, Chris Larsen, in 2012. It has both a currency and a payment system: the currency component is XRP, (has a mathematical foundation like Bitcoin), and the payment mechanism allows the transfer of funds, in any currency, to other users on the network within seconds (in contrast to Bitcoin transactions, which can take as long as 10 minutes to confirm).

MintChip - Unlike most cryptocurrencies, MintChip is actually the creation of a government institution, specifically the Royal Canadian Mint. MintChip is a smartcard that holds electronic value and can transfer it securely from one chip to another. Like Bitcoin, MintChip does not need personal identification; unlike Bitcoin, it is backed by a physical currency, the Canadian dollar.

Ethereum - The Ethereum project was born on the 30th July, 2015. It has been done by Vitalik Buterin, from Russia. Ethereum was designed for functionalities that Bitcoin and its alternatives can't provide—such as sending documents, text, pictures, software, etc. The Ethereum community is working on the developing of the project, on a daily basis. Their blockchain technology is the most advanced technology in the crypto world at this time, and many institutions are interested in it. The Ethereum blockchain is based on Smart contracts that determine functionalities of the subjects in the blockchain. Once the Smart contract is written and posted in the blockchain, it can't be modified, and stays there permanently.

*MPeso is not a cryptocurrency. It showed up in Nicaragua, in 2011, the first mobile money transfer and payment solution in the country.

In 2013, the company implemented a new digital fare-collection system for Managua's intra-city buses, using rechargeable contactless smart cards. All of the 834 city busses in Managua will be equipped with fare collection systems, and a total of 600,000 smart cards will be distributed.

Some of the limitations that cryptocurrencies presently face (one's digital fortune can be erased by a computer crash, or a virtual vault can be ransacked by a hacker) may be overcome in time, through technological advances. Harder to surmount is the basic paradox that bedevils cryptocurrencies: the more popular they become, the more regulation and government scrutiny they're likely to attract, which obviously diminishes the main premise for their existence.

And while the number of merchants who accept cryptocurrencies has steadily increased, they're still in the minority. There's also reason to believe their relative complexity, compared to conventional currencies, will likely deter most people (except for the technologically adept); however, people did get used to online banking and shopping, and that was once unimaginable.

| Notes |

CHAPTER 6
BITCOIN VERSUS ETHEREUM

| **Chapter 6** - Bitcoin versus Ethereum |

Released in 2009, Bitcoin has been the trailblazing leader of the cryptocurrency revolution. Numerous imitators have come and gone, but Bitcoin remains dominant, despite nearing the current limits of its transactional capacity. The following is a basic comparison of Bitcoin and its closest competitor, Ethereum …

	Bitcoin	**Ethereum**
• Created	2009	2015
• Market cap 9/11/2017	Over 68 billion	Over 27 billion
• Popular support	High	High
• Blockchain	Proof of work	Proof of work/Proof of stake
• Scalable	Not at the moment	Yes
• Mining	ASIC miners	GPUs
• Supply	21 million	81 million
• Development	Over 100 contributors	Small core team
• Hash rate 9/11/2017	Over 8.6 ExaHash	Over 100 TeraHash
• Initial distribution	Mining	ICO

Bitcoin and Ethereum are powered by the principle of distributed ledgers and cryptography, but they differ in many technical ways. Differences include block time. Ethereum transaction is confirmed in seconds, Bitcoin's in minutes. For their basic builds, Ethereum uses ethash, while Bitcoin uses the secure hash algorithm, SHA-256.

Bitcoin and Ethereum also differ in purpose. Bitcoin is created as an alternative to regular money and, therefore, is a medium of payment transaction and store of value. Ethereum is developed as a platform, which facilitates peer-to-peer contracts and applications, via its own currency vehicle. Both Bitcoin and Ethereum are digital currencies, but the primary purpose of Ethereum is to facilitate and monetize the working of Ethereum, to enable developers to build and run distributed applications (ÐApps).

Basically, Ethereum is an advancement based on the blockchain technology that supports Bitcoin, but with a purpose that does not compete with Bitcoin. However, the popularity and rising market capitalization of Ether brings it in competition with all cryptocurrencies, especially from the trading perspective. Currently, the market cap of Ether (ETH) is more than Ripple and Litecoin, although it's far behind Bitcoin (BTC). On the whole, Bitcoin and Ethereum are different versions using the blockchain technology, and are set to establish themselves, driven by different intentions.

| Notes |

CHAPTER 7
HOW TO GET CRYPTOCURRENCY/ CRYPTOCURRENCY EXCHANGES

| **Chapter 7 -** How to Get Cryptocurrency/ Cryptocurrency Exchanges |

You could mine your own bitcoins, but it is not an easy process. Bitcoins are mined, or searched for, by using computing processing power in a distributed network, to locate and solve mathematical problems to acquire the code for the coin. Also, there will be only 21 million bitcoins created, and roughly 16.8 million, or 80 percent of all the bitcoins, have already been mined. So, unlike the paper currencies in the world today, no governing body can print more bitcoin to dilute its value.

This means, for most people, the starting place will be to find a cryptocurrency exchange

Cryptocurrency exchanges are websites where you can buy, sell, or exchange cryptocurrencies for other digital currency, or traditional currency, like US dollars, British Pounds, or Euro. If you want to trade professionally, and have access to fancy trading tools, you'll probably need to use an exchange that requires you to open an account and verify your ID. Should you only want to make an occasional trade, there are also platforms you can use that don't require an account.

| **Types of exchanges** |

- **Trading Platforms –** These are website transactions.

- **Direct Trading** **–** These platforms offer direct, person-to-person trading of currency across many different countries. They don't have a fixed market price. Instead, each seller formulates their own exchange rate.

- **Brokers –** These are websites where anyone can visit to buy cryptocurrencies at a price set by the broker. Cryptocurrency brokers are similar to foreign exchange dealers.

There are some important things you should look into before making your first trade.

- **Reputation –** In order to find out about an exchange, search for reviews from individual users on well-known industry websites. For example, you can ask any questions you might have on forums like BitcoinTalk or Reddit.

- **Fees –** Exchanges should display fee-related information on their websites. Take time to make sure you understand deposit, transaction and withdrawal fees. They can differ substantially depending on which exchange you use.

- **Payment Methods –** Does the exchange offer lots of payment methods? Credit and debit card? Wire transfer? PayPal? If an exchange has limited payment options, then it may not be convenient for you to use it. Remember that purchasing cryptocurrencies with a credit card will always require identity verification and will come at a cost (as there is a higher risk of fraud). It will also result in higher transaction and processing fees. Purchasing cryptocurrency via wire transfer takes significantly longer due to bank processing times.

- **Verification Requirements –** The majority of Bitcoin trading platforms, both in the US and the UK, require some sort of ID verification in order to make deposits and withdrawals. Some exchanges, however, will allow you to remain anonymous. Just remember, although verification might seem like a pain, it protects the exchange against all sorts of scams and money laundering.

- **Geographical Restrictions –** Some functions offered by exchanges are only accessible from certain countries. Ensure the exchange allows full access to all platform tools and functions in the country you're living in.

- **Exchange Rate –** Different exchanges have different rates. Shop around and you could save yourself 10% or more.

There are a host of platforms to choose from, but not all exchanges are created equal. The following list is based on user reviews, user-friendliness, accessibility, fees, security, etcetera. It represents the 10 best exchanges, in no specific order.

| Coinbase |

Backed by trusted investors, and used by millions of customers, Coinbase is one of the most popular and well-known brokers and trading platforms in the world. You can securely buy, use, store and trade digital currency. Users can purchase Bitcoins, Ether and Litecoin through a digital wallet available on both Android and iPhone, or through trading with other users on the company's Global Digital Asset Exchange (GDAX) subsidiary. GDAX operates in the US, Europe, UK, Canada, Australia and Singapore. GDAX does not charge any transfer fees for moving funds between your Coinbase account and GDAX account. The selection of tradable currencies will, however, depend on the country you live in.

- **Pros:** good reputation, security, reasonable fees, beginner-friendly and stored currency is covered by Coinbase insurance.

- **Cons:** customer support, limited payment methods, limited countries supported, non-uniform rollout of services worldwide and GDAX suitable for technical traders only.

| Kraken |

As the biggest Bitcoin exchange in euro volume and liquidity, Kraken is a partner in the first cryptocurrency bank. It lets you buy and sell bitcoins and trade between bitcoins and euros, US Dollars, Canadian Dollars, British Pounds, and Japanese Yen. Kraken also makes it possible to trade digital currencies other than Bitcoin. Some of these are Augur, Dogecoin, Ethereum, Ethereum Classic, ICONOMI, Litecoin, Monero, REP tokens, Ripple, Stellar/Lumens and Zcash.

For more experienced users, Kraken offers margin trading and a host of other trading features.

- **Pros:** good reputation, decent exchange rates, low transaction fees, minimal deposit fees, feature rich, great user support, secure and supported worldwide.

- **Cons:** limited payment methods, not suitable for beginners and unintuitive user interface.

| Cex.io |

Cex.io provides a large number of services for using Bitcoin and other cryptocurrencies. The platform also allows users to easily trade fiat money with cryptocurrencies and, conversely, cryptocurrencies for fiat money. For professionals, the platform offers personalized and easy-to-use trading dashboards and margin trading. CEX also offers a brokerage service that provides novice traders a simple way to buy bitcoin at prices that are in line with the market rate. The Cex.io website is secure and intuitive, and cryptocurrencies can be stored in safe, cold storage.

- **Pros:** good reputation, good mobile product, supports credit cards, beginner-friendly, decent exchange rate and is supported worldwide.

- **Cons:** average customer support, drawn out verification process and depositing is expensive.

| ShapeShift |

ShapeShift supports a variety of cryptocurrencies, including Bitcoin, Dash, Dogecoin, Ethereum, Monero, Zcash, and many others. Shapeshift is terrific for those who want to make instant and straightforward trades, without signing up for an account or relying on a platform to hold their funds. ShapeShift doesn't allow users to purchase cryptos with debit cards, credit cards, or any other payment system. The platform has a no-fiat policy and only allows for the exchange between bitcoin and the other supported cryptocurrencies.

- **Pros:** good reputation, beginner-friendly, dozens of cryptos available for exchange, fast and reasonable prices.

- **Cons:** average mobile app, no fiat currencies and limited payment options and tools.

| Poloniex |

The exchange offers a secure trading environment and has more than 100 Bitcoin cryptocurrency pairings. It features advanced tools and data analysis for advanced traders. With one of the highest trading volumes, its users will always be able to close a trade position. Poloniex features a volume-tiered, maker-taker fee schedule for all trades. This means fees are different for the maker and the taker. For makers, fees are available from 0 to 0.15%, depending on the amount traded. For takers, fees are a bit higher at 0.10 to 0.25%. There are no additional fees for withdrawals. The Poloniex platform also offers the chat box, which is constantly filled with user help. Beware, it can sometimes be hard to distinguish the good advice from the bad. However, the Chatbox is a great tool that will keep you engaged.

- **Pros:** fast account creation, feature rich BTC lending, high volume trading, user-friendly, low trading fees and open API.

- **Cons:** slow customer service and no fiat support.

| Bitstamp |

Bitstamp is a European Union based bitcoin marketplace. The platform is a first-generation bitcoin exchange that has built up a loyal customer base. Bitstamp is well-known and trusted as a safe platform. It offers advanced security features, like two-step authentication, multisig technology for its wallet and fully insured cold storage. Bitstamp has 24/7 support and a multilingual user interface. Getting started is easy: just open a free account, make a deposit and start trading right away.

- **Pros:** good reputation, high-level security, worldwide availability, low transaction fees and good for large transactions.

- **Cons:** not beginner-friendly, limited payment methods, high deposit fees and user interface.

| CoinMama |

Anyone can visit this veteran platform to buy Bitcoin or Ether, using your credit card, cash, MoneyGram and Western Union. CoinMama is terrific for those who want to make instant and straightforward purchases of digital currency, using their local currency. Although the service is available worldwide, some countries may not be able to use all the functions of the site. CoinMama operates in English, German, French, Italian, and Russian.

- **Pros:** good reputation, beginner-friendly, great user interface, good range of payment options, available worldwide and fast transaction time.

- **Cons:** high exchange rates, a premium fee for credit card, no bitcoin sell function and average user support.

| Bitsquare |

Bitsquare is a user-friendly, peer-to-peer exchange that allows you to buy and sell bitcoins in exchange for fiat currencies or cryptocurrencies. Bitsquare markets itself as a truly decentralized and peer-to-peer exchange that's instantly accessible. It requires no registration and doesn't rely on a central authority. Bitsquare never holds user funds, and no one except trading partners exchange personal data. The platform offers great security, with multisig addresses, security deposit, and an arbitrator system in case of trade disputes. If you want to remain anonymous, Bitsquare is the perfect platform for you.

- **Pros:** good reputation, secure and private. A vast amount of cryptocurrencies available, no sign-up, decent fees, open source, available worldwide and good for advanced traders.

- **Cons:** limited payment options, average customer support and not beginner-friendly.

| LocalBitcoin |

LocalBitcoin is a person-to-person Bitcoin exchange--with buyers and sellers in thousands of cities around the world. Using LocalBitcoins, you can meet up with people in your area and buy or sell bitcoins in cash, send money through PayPal, Skrill or Dwolla. You can even arrange to deposit cash at a bank branch. LocalBitcoin only takes a commission of 1% from the sellers who set their own exchange rates. The platform takes a number of precautions to ensure trading is secure. To begin with, LocalBitcoin sets each trader with a reputation rank, publicly displaying past activities. Once a trade is requested, the money is held on LocalBitcoins' escrow service. When the seller confirms the trade, the funds are released. If something happens to go wrong, LocalBitcoins has a support team to resolve conflicts between buyers and sellers.

- **Pros:** no ID required, beginner-friendly, usually free, instant transfers and available worldwide..

- **Cons:** hard to buy large numbers of bitcoin and high exchange rates.

| Gemini |

Co-founded by Tyler and Cameron Winklevoss, Gemini is a fully regulated, licensed US Bitcoin and Ether exchange. That means Gemini's capital requirements and regulatory standards are similar to a bank. Also, all US dollar deposits are held at a FDIC-insured bank, and the majority of digital currency is held in cold storage. Gemini trades in three currencies—US dollars, bitcoin, and ether—which means the platform doesn't serve traders of the countless of other cryptocurrencies. The exchange operates using a maker-taker fee schedule, with discounts available for high volume traders. Deposits and withdrawals are free of charge. The platform is fully available in 42 US states, Canada, Hong Kong, Japan, Singapore, South Korea and the UK.

- **Pros:** security and compliance, slick/minimalistic and user-friendly design, great analytics and high liquidity.

- **Cons:** limited currencies, small community, average customer support, limited worldwide availability and no margin trading.

BTW - by the time you are reading topics about exchanges and providers mentioned above, they can already have new features. Note that new providers/exchanges are coming to the markets. This list is only for figurative purposes to give you a picture of the possibilities.

| Acquiring a wallet |

A wallet is much like a bank account that can reside on your computer, phone or other smart device. It's always advisable to have your wallet backed up in another location so that a crashed hard drive does not wipe out your (bit) coins.

There are many wallet types. What you choose will depend on your security needs and whether you wish to be an active trader or a more passive buy-and-hold investor.

Once you've set up your wallet, then you can go to one of the many digital currency exchanges to purchase a bitcoin. (There also exists alternative options where cryptocurrencies can be bought.)

Many exchanges now allow you to buy bitcoins with a credit card or debit card. Web.Coinbase.com, and Coindesk.com, are two of the largest cryptocurrency platforms. They offer tutorials on digital currencies.

If you don't wish to use your bank account, there's one site, called LocalBitcoins.com, which allows face-to-face purchases.

Cryptocurrencies are easy to get into, and they're versatile and resilient, even to serious drops in the economy. They're also growing by the day and aren't going away anytime soon; in fact, they're likely to grow until they become an integrated part of our monetary systems—not just on a small scale, but globally. Cryptocurrencies, such as Bitcoin, are already accepted in stores that you can actually walk into. Imagine what it'll be like when such transactions are normal.

| Notes |

| Notes |

CHAPTER 8
WHAT IS THE MINING OF CRYPTOCURRENCY?

| **Chapter 8 -** What is the Mining of Cryptocurrency? |

Mining is the contributing your computer resources to ensure the transactions on the Bitcoin network (or any other coin's network) are authentic. In layman's terms, miners volunteer their computers to ensure that all activity on the network is clean. In exchange for this, miners are rewarded with coins.

Cloud mining is where you're not using your own computer. Instead, you're renting hardware offered by someone else who agrees to share the rewards.

Where do bitcoins come from? With Bitcoin, miners utilize special software to solve complicated math problems. They're issued a certain number of bitcoins in exchange. This provides a clever way to issue the currency and also creates an incentive for more people to mine.

Bitcoin miners help to keep the Bitcoin network secure by using their computers to approve transactions. Mining is a fundamental part of Bitcoin and ensures fairness while keeping the Bitcoin network stable, safe, and secure.

Currently, based on price per hash and electrical efficiency, the best Bitcoin miner options are AntMiner S7, AntMiner S9, and Avalon6.

Bitcoin mining is the process that adds transaction records to a public ledger of past transactions. This ledger is called the blockchain, as it is a chain of blocks. The blockchain serves to confirm transactions, to the rest of the network, as having taken place.

Bitcoin nodes use the blockchain to distinguish legitimate Bitcoin transactions from attempts to re-spend coins that have already been spent elsewhere.

Bitcoin mining is designed to be resource-intensive and difficult, so that the number of blocks found each day remains steady. Each valid block contains a verified proof of work. Bitcoin nodes provide this verification each time they receive a block. The hashcash proof-of-work function is used by all.

First and foremost, mining allows Bitcoin nodes to reach a secure, tamper-resistant consensus. Mining also introduces Bitcoins into the system: miners are paid transaction fees, as well as a subsidy of newly created coins. This disseminates new coins in a decentralized manner and motivates people to provide security for the Bitcoin system.

Bitcoin mining resembles the mining of other commodities. Exertion is required, and new currency is made available at a rate that resembles the way gold, for example, is mined from the ground.

A proof of work is a piece of data that was difficult (costly and time-consuming) to produce, so as to satisfy certain requirements. It must be easy to check whether data satisfies the requirements.

Producing a proof of work is a low probability process, so that much trial and error is usually required before a valid proof is generated.

Bitcoin mining a block is difficult because the SHA-256 hash of a block's header must start with a certain number of zeros. The probability of calculating such a hash is low, therefore many attempts must be made. To generate a new hash each round, something called a nonce is incremented. See proof of work for more information.

The Bitcoin mining network difficulty is the measure of how difficult it is to find a new block, compared to the easiest it can ever be. It's recalculated, every 2016 blocks, to a value such that the previous 2016 blocks would have been generated in just two weeks--had everyone been mining at this difficulty. The average yield would then be one block per ten minutes.

More miners mean the rate of block creation will go up. As the rate goes up, the difficulty rises to compensate, which will push the rate back down. Any blocks (like those released by malicious miners) that don't meet the set difficulty target will be rejected by everyone on the network, making such blocks worthless.

When a block is discovered, the discoverer may award themselves a certain number of bitcoins, which is agreed upon by everyone in the network. Currently, this bounty is 12 bitcoins; this value will halve, every 210,000 blocks.

Additionally, the miner is awarded the fees paid by users sending transactions. The fee is meant to motivate the miner to include the transaction in their block. In the future, as the number of new bitcoins that miners are allowed to create in each block dwindles, the fees will make up a much more important percentage of mining income.

| Notes |

| Notes |

CHAPTER 9
HOW TO MINE CRYPTOCURRENCY

| Chapter 9 - How to Mine Cryptocurrency |

To do this, you need to buy expensive equipment, and have the know-how. Mining cryptocurrency is also speculative in nature. So, while it can be an enjoyable pastime, one needs to assess the risks involved in this type of mining: time, labour, and money.

Another easy way you can acquire cryptocurrency is to go to an exchange, of which there are many (just do an online search for cryptocurrency exchanges). Some of these websites allow exchange by fiat (the US Dollar, for example). It's as simple as opening an account and sending the currency to your bank account, credit card, or debit card.

Then there is the option of just holding the currency as an investment. There is no guarantee the value of the currency you choose will go up.

You can also exchange goods and services for the cryptocurrency (e.g., Bitcoin or Ethereum).

You can even create your own coin, but you must know what to do with it and/or why people would use it.

| Proof of work vs Proof of stake: |

Proof of work – You can only mine cryptocurrencies that are of the proof of work type. In other words, the computer, hardware, and program(s) you are using to mine a cryptocurrency should show proof of work done. This is a person-to-person network that has come together for the purpose of mining a specific cryptocurrency by finding blocks for the blockchain. An example would be when you are rewarded 12 bitcoins for proving a new block of cryptocurrency actually went to an end user. The best way to do this is to find and enlist the help of the best miners in the business.

When Bitcoin first began, there was supposed to be a new block of 50 coins discovered every 10 minutes, but as the cryptocurrency has a limited or finite number of blocks that can be discovered (no more will ever be issued), this increment is actually being halved over certain periods of time. So, today, we are actually receiving only 12 bitcoins for each new block added to the Bitcoin blockchain. When six different confirmations of a particular block of transactions come in, then the confirmation of the block is considered confirmed. Most companies are using just two transactions.

Proof of stake – They have coins that are pre-mined and given to the blockchain that will pay a reward or share a stake.

| How it started |

Bitcoin was the first cryptocurrency, and it was intended that you could mine for blocks using your own computer processor, with your own graphic card (in 2009). Then, people discovered if they put together a group of graphic cards, there would be a greater chance that they would find blocks. Over time, they produced the one computer with the chip size needed to do the job. This machine, however, was very power hungry, and proved to be too expensive to operate. So, the computer world got together with the crypto world, and designed an ASIC machine that has no other function but to mine; but the development of such a machine could cost upward of a million dollars. However, you can put the hash rate up independently by putting together different graphic cards.

| Why mining? |

If no one is mining a specific cryptocurrency, then none will be available; and because no one is confirming transactions (the entire purpose of blockchain), no one will want to buy the coins. The only way to kill a cryptocurrency is, in fact, to stop mining it. The miners are keeping cryptocurrency stable, safe, and secure.

| Notes |

CHAPTER 10
BLOCKCHAIN
TECHNOLOGY

| **Chapter 10 -** Blockchain Technology |

Satoshi Nakamoto, active in the develpment of Bircoin until December 2010, is an unknown person, or persons, who designed Bitcoin, and created its original reference implementation. He also devised the first blockchain database and solved the double spending problem for digital currency.

Nakamoto has claims he lives in Japan and was born on April 5, 1975. Most people, however, suspect he is a cryptography and computer science expert of non-Japanese descent, living in the United States and Europe.

As of May 24, 2017, Nakamoto is believed to own up to roughly one million bitcoins, with a value estimated at approximately $2.7 billion USD.

| **What is a Blockchain?** |

A blockchain is a public ledger of all Bitcoin transactions that have ever been executed. Blocks to the chain in a linear and chronological order. Each node (a computer connected to the Bitcoin network that allows a client to validate and relay transactions) automatically gets a copy of the blockchain upon joining the Bitcoin network. The blockchain stores each and every transaction address and balance.

A block stores recent transaction, and once completed goes into the blockchain permanently. A new block is then generated. Each block is linked to another (like a chain), with every block containing a hash of the previous block.

Think of the blockchain as a full history of banking transactions. Bitcoin transactions are entered chronologically in a blockchain, just the way bank transactions are. Blocks, meanwhile, are like individual bank statements.

The Bitcoin blockchain database is shared by all nodes participating in the system. The full copy of the blockchain has records of every Bitcoin transaction ever executed.

The ever-growing size of the blockchain is becoming a problem due to issues like storage and synchronization. On an average, every 10 minutes, a new block is appended to the blockchain through mining.

Because the validation of any recording on the blockchain isn't centralized, it eliminates the need of a third-party to an intermediate. There's an irrevocable trail of all the transactions that have ever been made, which makes hacking or fraud unlikely. Because of this, the blockchain allows work to be done at lower costs, with greater regulatory compliance, reduced risk, and enhanced efficiency.

Banks were among the first to look at blockchain technology as a platform that offers them unparalleled cost advantages and efficiency. In fact, as many as 40 banks have formed a consortium that they claim has successfully completed a ground-breaking, distributed ledger experiment.

Blockchain technology can help to decrease the time it takes to settle a trade. The current system takes 3 days from transaction (stocks, corporate bonds, municipal securities, and mutual funds shares), while a few require two days (foreign exchange settlements), or one day (treasury bonds). Institutions have been attempting to condense the time it takes for each trade, thus decreasing counter-party risk. Smart contracts may provide a solution. Goldman Sachs has already filed a patent application for a cryptographic currency protocol-based settlement system for the securities market. The technology is also being tested to improve transparency and functioning of back-office for securities. NASDAQ has its own blockchain technology and has used it to document the issuance of shares.

Blockchain technology can also be used in the insurance sector, which needs to maintain gigantic records of premiums, claims, and payments. The industry faces great threat from fraud, such as crash for cash, which are scams run by fraudsters who manufacture collisions, sometimes with innocent road users, hoping to profit from fraudulent insurance claims. With claims from a single collision potentially worth ten of thousands of dollars, organized fraudsters are orchestrating scams that involve multiple collisions, and can be worth millions of dollars.

The blockchain can help to make the public-sector service more efficient by plugging the loopholes; matters such as citizen identity, vehicle registry, pensions, tax payments, patents, and assets (real estate) can be registered on the blockchain. Additionally, industries such as media, diamond, music, and healthcare have already started tapping blockchain technology.

The diamond industry faces its own unique problems, like insurance fraud, and tracking the origin of diamonds: it has struggled to track and check the entry of blood diamonds from entering the legitimate supply chain of diamonds. Everledger is using blockchain technology to tackle these problems, defining itself as a "fraud detection system, overlaying big data from closed sources, like insurers and law enforcement."

Companies like PeerTracks, Bittunes, and Ujo Music have been working to bring the blockchain technology to the music industry, to resolve the problem of monetizing music in an easy and convenient way.

Although the blockchain technology is just making its debut in many spheres of business and industry, there are signs that it is here to stay. This technology, which is the backbone of Bitcoin and other virtual currencies, is being endorsed and praised by prominent institutions, from the International Monetary Fund (IMF) to government advisory bodies. What does all this mean? Blockchain technology may prove to be a great disrupter to the traditional banking industry and is thus being taken seriously by the major players.

The tamper-proof, decentralized, immutable nature of the blockchain make it ideal for reducing costs and streamlining everything from payments, asset trading, securities issuance, retail banking, and clearing, and settlements. It becomes obvious that blockchain technology is much more than Bitcoin or cryptocurrencies. While those implementations as payments and money systems are indeed disruptive, the greater disruption may come from alternative uses of these unique and powerful characteristics.

SegWit (Segregated Witness) is a proposed update to the Bitcoin software (Bitcoin Core), designed to fix a range of serious issues. The update is designed to solve transaction malleability, a well-known weak spot in Bitcoin software. There have already been several attacks, underlining the need for the patch.

SegWit also offers a range of other advantages, and the focus of attention has shifted from fixing the transaction malleability, to solving the problem of Bitcoin scaling. Bitcoin is currently experiencing massive scaling problems, which are only getting worse with time.

What is SegWit's solution to the Bitcoin scaling problem? SegWit increases the Bitcoin's block size limit and allows the implementation of second-layer solutions for further improvement. Current issues of Bitcoin scalability arise primarily from the insufficient block size. Consecutive blocks of transactions are what the Blockchain is comprised of. The Blockchain, in turn, is the ledger of all transactions that have taken place in the network up until now—the lifeblood of the cryptocurrency.

The problem here is that blocks currently have a hard-coded limit of one megabyte. This is not enough to allow for the accounting of the hundreds of transactions that occur every minute.

Consequently, a lot of users have to wait to have their transaction confirmed--for hours or even days. As the network grows, so does the transaction intensity. Unfortunately, the block size limit always stays the same, resulting in a problem that's getting worse.

SegWit offers two solutions. First, it enables an immediate increase of the block size limit to four megabytes. This will be the maximum size. Secondly, by solving transaction malleability, SegWit removes a major barrier to implementing second-layer solutions. One such solution is the proposed Lightning Network, which is expected to allow for a massive increase in the network capacity by moving the bulk of transactions off the Blockchain for quick processing.

| Notes |

| Notes |

CHAPTER 11
CRYPTOCURRENCY PAYMENT POSSIBILITIES

| **Chapter 11 -** Cryptocurrency Payment Possibilities |

As I mentioned before, there are many possibilities for payments with cryptocurrencies.

In the beginning, there were few merchants that accepted Bitcoins as a payment. Today, we can say there are endless possibilities to pay with bitcoins and other acceptable cryptocurrencies. There is no limit to do that.

At the beginning, the only way to pay with cryptocurrency was by changing goods or services for BTC by physically sending from one BTC address to another. Then, the buyer received the purchased good or service. I believe that this was the real Satoshi Nakamoto's vision with exchanging goods for goods. That's what BTC is meant for. The best-known example of an exchanged good for BTC is a famous pizza deal, where one guy offered 20,000 BTC for two pizzas. He said if somebody ordered two pizzas and sent them to his home address, then he would send 20,000 BTC to the guy. And you won't believe it: one guy showed up and sent the two pizzas. If this guy had held onto those BTC until today, he would be a multi-millionaire!

Of course, today, there is still the possibility to exchange cryptocurrency for goods in this way. But with a bigger need of cryptocurrency payments, and tremendous growth in value, new possibilities of payments have arrived to support this market.

BTC growth of popularity came with the BTC cash machines, or BTC ATMs, where customers buy or sell their BTC with or for cash. By inserting money in the ATM, somebody can buy BTC with the real-time BTC price (exchange price) or sell BTC by sending BTC to a unique address shown in the ATM and take out cash from the machine. The only bad side of these machines is a high fee for the service (up to 10%). But with the big BTC price fluctuations, we are seeing that this 10% can often be ignored. In my opinion, this is still one of the best ways to cash out BTC.

One of the biggest game changers in this industry was when VISA accepted to cooperate with online BTC providers like Bitpay, Cryptopay, Xapo, and many others. They were offering a service where you can open an account and use it for storing BTC. You can use them as a regular online wallet by sending or receiving BTC. And when you want or need to spend your BTC, you can simply do it through your debit card. You make the purchase, and the provider simply exchanges your BTC in a card currency (USD, EUR, GBP, or other fiat currencies). Of course, they take some fees for the service. But the simplicity of the usage in this way, for the customer, is really fantastic. The same is with ATM withdrawals. They work in the same way.

With the need for online shops to accept cryptocurrency BTC, or other cryptocurrency payments, the software developers created many different programs and apps to facilitate this process. Today, you can pay with your cryptocurrency in a million places, online and offline. And with the growth of the cryptocurrency popularity, this number is growing every day. There is software developed for small shops with not so many transactions and, of course, there is software that allows for bigger number of transactions.

We call them Customized Cryptocurrency Processors. Mostly, we use them for people or companies who have their own cryptocurrency, or they simply have to accept or send multiple cryptocurrency transactions.

The processors are working like a bank or as a provider for transactions. So, if you are a big merchant, you can use them to allow the customer to pay with bitcoin, Ethereum, etc. The system will automatically notify the vendor when the payment is verified or rejected. The fee from CoinDesk is approximately 4% for Bitcoin.
Together with our IT team, we built a very efficient processor. A friend of ours wanted to start a small business using Bitcoin as currency (pay in/pay out). We set him up with the processor, and he was very happy. The block explorer will show every transaction, for every day, including the fee charged by the processor. It even shows purchases that were never paid for.

There is no limitation; such processors can be built and customized for every existing cryptocurrency, depending on the customer need. **For more information regarding Customized Cryptocurrency Processors, please contact Dejan Deki Markovic at cryptocurrenciesbook@gmail.com.**

It is possible to send 1,000 transactions per minute with current Bitcoin processors, but this rate will improve with the need. Etherium can process even more. Customized processors are used for people who have their own cryptocurrency, for example. And, of course, there are brokers.

Contact Deki for more information at cryptocurrenciesbook@ gmail.com

Most crypto investors still trade with exchanges directly, which raises the question: what is the need for a broker at all? There are several answers emanating from the issue of user experience.

Most cryptocurrency exchanges weren't built with a simple trading experience in mind. As such, they offer cumbersome interfaces, little support for third party platforms, and very limited customer support options.

If you've ever tried to contact one of the bigger exchanges, with a problem that needed active support, you likely only received canned email responses that felt like you were corresponding with a cheap chat robot. A good broker offers great client support so that, for example, if you forget your password, you won't completely lose your account, as can happen with an exchange.

Online brokers usually have about twenty years of experience with trading, developing platforms, and ancillary services, while the cryptocurrency ecosystem is still in its infancy. If you're used to trading on the charts, from a mobile app, or need all your EA robots for algo trading, a broker is the way to go.

BROKER	LEVERAGE	BITCOIN	ETHEREUM	LITECOIN	DASH	RIPPLE
Plus500	up to 1:30	✔	✔	✔	✔	✔
FxOpen	up to 1:3	✔	✔	✔	✔	✘
UFX	1:4	✔	✔	✘	✘	✘
Markets	up to 1:10	✔	✔	✔	✔	✔
IG	1:13	✔	✔	✘	✘	✘
SimpleFX	up to 1:10	✔	✔	✔	✘	✔
Evolve Markets	up to 1:25	✔	✔	✔	✘	✘
1Broker	N/A	✔	✘	✘	✘	✘
ForexClub	up to 1:20	✔	✘	✔	✘	✘
Bulltraders	N/A	✔	✘	✘	✘	✘
Whaleclub	up to 1:20	✔	✔	✔	✔	✘
Forexee	1:3	✔	✔	✔	✔	✘
FXCortex	N/A	✔	✘	✘	✘	✘
Alpari	up to 1:10	✔	✘	✘	✘	✘
Admiral Markets	1:5	✔	✔	✔	✘	✔
Exante	N/A	✔	✔	✔	✘	✔
Trade360	1:4	✔	✔	✘	✘	✘
HotForex	1:20	✔	✘	✘	✘	✘
IFM Trade	up to 1:16	✔	✔	✔	✔	✔
AvaTrade	1:50	✔	✘	✘	✘	✘
FXPRIMUS	1:5	✔	✔	✔	✔	✔

BROKER	LEVERAGE	BITCOIN	ETHEREUM	LITECOIN	DASH	RIPPLE
HYCM	1:20	✔	✔	✔	✘	✘
IQ Options	1:1	✔	✔	✔	✔	✔
Trade	1:20	✔	✔	✔	✔	✔
Vantage FX	1:1	✔	✘	✘	✘	✘
InstaForex	1:10	✔	✘	✘	✘	✘
NordFX	1:3	✔	✔	✔	✘	✘
796	N/A	✔	✘	✘	✘	✘
PrivateFX	N/A	✔	✘	✘	✘	✘
1billionforex	1:3	✔	✘	✘	✘	✘
Salma Markets	1:1	✔	✘	✘	✘	✘
Ayondo	1:7	✔	✘	✘	✘	✘
FXChoice	1:3	✔	✘	✘	✘	✘
Fortrade	1:5	✔	✔	✔	✔	✘
AAAFx	N/A	✔	✔	✔	+	✘
HYCM	1:10	✔	✘	✘	✘	✘
SwissQuote	1:1	✔	✘	✘	✘	✘
JFD Brokers	1:10	✔	✘	✘	✘	✘
XTB	up to 1:20	✔	✔	✔	✔	✔
AvaTrade	up to 1:20	✔	✔	✔	✔	✔
peToro	1:1	✔	✔	✔	✔	✔

Crypto exchanges have also fallen victim to cyber-attacks, exit scams, and FBI takedowns. While everyone can be hacked, at least a broker, who you know and trust, can provide some accountability in case anything goes wrong.

FX Brokers are adding cryptocurrencies because of volatility. While long-term investors can just buy an asset at an exchange, transfer it to a secure wallet and hold, day traders look for something else. Volatility creates many small trading opportunities, which they try to capture with risking holding for long term. As such, crypto assets are magnets for short-term and algo forex traders.

The major fiat currency pairs offer volatility that is literally thousands of times less than cryptocurrencies, so they cannot match the excitement associated with trading them.

Incredible hype surrounds Bitcoin and Ethereum in the mainstream financial media, and many clients are demanding access to them. By offering a few more CFDs (Contract for Differences), a broker can reach a huge new market, one with no desire to ever use blockchain assets for anything else.

Bitcoin trading has been supported by brokers for a few years now but saw an explosion in the number of cryptocurrency offerings this year. The incredible rally in blockchain asset prices has attracted so many new companies to the crypto bandwagon—how does a trader choose who to go with?

To help, Finance Magnates have assembled the ultimate list of brokers offering cryptocurrency trading. We examined which top currencies they support, and what the offered leverage is, so you can review the whole market in one place.

| Notes |

CHAPTER 12
WHY TO HOLD CRYPTOCURRENCY

| **Chapter 12 -** Why to Hold Cryptocurrency |

Cryptocurrency values are volatile at best. To try and trade Bitcoin, for example, you are working in the short term, which has proven to be more like gambling than investing. No, the best way to approach any cryptocurrency is to take a small part of your portfolio, try to buy low, and then hang onto it over the long term. It isn't as exhilarating as day trading cryptocurrencies, but it is the best system, as proved time and again on the current stock markets.

Cryptocurrencies are worth what people are willing to pay, which should increase over time, as creators and investors believe. But like stocks, cryptocurrencies will plunge in price if everyone starts to sell. Where the real value will come out, however, is when cryptocurrencies can be exchanged for (goods and services) other than the fiat system.

There is another reason why somebody should hold cryptocurrency. But in the first place, we have to understand how the holding of the cryptocurrency is affecting the market.

The first thing to understand is the capitalization of the cryptocurrency. If you check on the coinmarketcap.com webpage, you will find all the statistics and values of all officially recognized cryptocurrency. At the top of the page, you will also find the capitalization of all cryptocurrency, expressed in USD (fiat). This amount is a calculation from a total supply of cryptocurrency in the circulation, and a singular average unit price of each cryptocurrency. So, this is the fiat money quantity if everyone were to sell all the supply of all cryptocurrency, at the same time. Of course, somebody should pay for it as well. As you have now discovered, this is an impossible process, and is only theoretical.

The truth is, in the market, there is only a few % of the fiat money for cryptocurrency exchanges. The rest is theoretical. If you want to get the real picture of the fiat money in cryptocurrency, then you should calculate the daily volume of trading of all cryptocurrency together. This is quite accurate detail regarding the fiat money spent in cryptocurrency.

But, what do I want to say with this? It is simple. Mostly, the value of the cryptocurrency is growing because of those people who are not selling but holding. We call them Crypto holders. If you don't put so much supply on the market, and the demand is growing, then the price is going up—it's a law of nature. If the held supply will come out in the market for selling, and if the capital will not come in parallel, then the price will go down drastically.

But, if we have a huge cryptocurrency market, who do we have to thank? Both! Those who are investing new capital in the cryptocurrency market, and those who are not selling (the Crypto holders). And who are the Crypto holders? Mostly, these people are from the cryptocurrency world: software builders, crypto idealists, cryptocurrency lovers…or just cryptocurrency believers, who believe in a decentralized, meritocratic, non-corrupt and fair financial system.

| Should you invest in cryptocurrencies? |

If you're considering investing in cryptocurrencies, you may want to treat your investment like any other highly speculative venture. In other words, recognize that you run the risk of losing most of your investment, if not all of it. As stated earlier, a cryptocurrency has no intrinsic value, apart from what a buyer is willing to pay for it when you want to sell. This makes it susceptible to huge price swings, which in turn increases the risk of loss for an investor—especially if he doesn't have time to wait for the market to go up again. Bitcoin, for example, plunged from $260 to about $130, within a six-hour period, on April 11, 2013. If you can't stomach this kind of volatility, look elsewhere for investments better suited to you. Supporters of Bitcoin point to its limited supply and growing usage as a value driver. Detractors see it as just another speculative bubble. This is a debate that a conservative investor would do well to avoid.

But for those who have a visionary mind, cryptocurrency investment can bring a fortune. (E.g., Bitcoin's starting price was $0.10; today, the price overpassed $4000 per piece.) Imagine if you had invested $1000 at that time; now, you would have a worth of $40,000,000— not bad.

But before you invest, my suggestion is to acquire some knowledge regarding crypto, and how to do it in a safe way. And remember, do not invest the last money that you will need for living. Always use the money that you know you will not miss; what's really important is that at night you can sleep peacefully! When people are too nervous, it is more likely they will make mistakes and bad decisions.

Blockchain technology is probably the hottest trend in finance, with the potential to completely transform traditional business models in a number of sectors. Blockchain is like a massive digital spreadsheet that is shared by the members of a decentralized network. While blockchain technology is best known for confirming Bitcoin payments, it can also be used in a number of other ways. Bitcoin has been valued at almost $70 billion so far.

Along with a rapidly expanding user base, Bitcoin is being considered by a number of financial services companies. The of major benefit now offered by cryptocurrency is the reduction cost of transferring funds, especially on a global scale. The impact of Bitcoin technology on the finance industry has been likened to the disruption that the Internet caused in the music and publishing industries.

In light of such tremendous promise, investors have begun to look at how they can tap into the profit potential of blockchain technology. Given the nature of blockchain technology, prior to making any investment decisions, there are certain unique factors to consider. On the other hand, opportunities for investing in blockchain technology abound, giving all investors a chance to leverage the potential this revolutionary technology offers. How you invest in blockchain technology will largely depend on the amount of risk you are willing to accept, as well as the type of yield you wish to achieve.

Stockpiling Bitcoin. Just as many investors have stockpiled gold, in anticipation of the rising price, other investors are taking advantage of the opportunity to stockpile Biitcoins. Yes, gold is a tangible item and Bitcoin is not, but many of the basic investment principles remain the same. For example, both are considered rare. And while the rate at which Bitcoins were generated in the early days of the technology was relatively fast, that rate has slowed over the last few years as the technology reaches a built-in limit of 21 million coins

It all about supply and demand. As demand for Bitcoins increases, value also rises. And with more methods for procuring Bitcoin being made available, there has never been a better time to begin a cryptocurrency investment portfolio.

Cryptocurrency Penny Stocks. While Bitcoin is the most well-known digital currency, it's certainly not the only option. Other types include Litecoin and Altcoins. Some of these digital currencies were developed in an attempt to compete with Bitcoin, but many others were designed to fill needs not met by Bitcoin. For instance, some cryptocurrencies have been developed for the purposes of enabling digital asset registry, providing increased privacy, allowing escrow services, and more. Bitcoin penny stocks, like Bitcoin Shop Inc., Global Future City Holding, and American Green, Inc., offer Bitcoin penny stock investment opportunities.

Crowdfunding is considered to be a popular mainstream method for raising seed capital for all types of investments. If you're looking to get involved in blockchain technology, one way is through a crowdfunding method that uses alternative coins. With this method, the total coin supply is pre-mined. Then it's sold in an initial coin offering, or ICO, prior to the network being publicly launched. Bitshares is just one of many coin networks that used crowdfunding to get started. Services and apps using blockchain technology have also used this pre-sale method to raise funding. Investors have the opportunity to purchase coins, with the expectation that prices will increase at some point in the future--if the service becomes popular.

Angel funding and investing in start-ups aren't new concepts. One variation that is gaining traction is the idea of investing in start-ups built on blockchain technology. As Bitcoin has become more mainstream, the number of entrepreneurs experimenting with the technology supporting the cryptocurrency has skyrocketed. Such start-ups need funding. Providing start-up and angel funding gets you in on the ground floor of what could be the next Google, Apple or internet. Of course, it should be understood that there are significant risks in such investments. Since the profit potential is massive, it is important to carefully weigh both the pros and the cons.

Pure Blockchain Technology. Companies such as hashing Space Corporation, BTCS, Inc. and Global Arena Holding are rapidly becoming well-known names in the arena of blockchain technology. BTCS, for example, is considered by many as the first pure play United States public company focused on the blockchain technology. It works to secure the blockchain through its distinctive transaction verification services. Global Arena Holding is leveraging blockchain technology for its potential in voting verification.

Not sure which investment method is right for your risk profile? If you want to keep risk low, your best option is to invest in stocks issued by one of the large financial services companies that are experimenting with the potential of blockchain technology to improve services. For investors who have a higher tolerance of risk, investing in one of the pure blockchain technology investment opportunities could deliver the right combination of risk versus return.

While many naysayers contend that blockchain technology and cryptocurrencies such as Bitcoin are just a passing fad, six years in they represent a concept that continues to gain steam and could even have the power to change the world. For those adventurous investors who choose to become involved in the blockchain technology boom, the payoff could be massive.

Can I have my own cryptocurrency? (There is more information on this topic, under Finally, My Own Cryptocurrency)

Bitcoin may have become a thing of fascination for the media very recently, but the digital currency actually celebrated its fifth birthday during the month when its value came in at about $1,000 per coin.

Bitcoin wasn't ever intended to be the one cryptocurrency to rule them all--anyone can make their own version of it. The code for the currency was released via an open-source licence. This means anyone can use it and alter any aspect they wish, in order to create a whole new currency!

A whole class of alternative cryptocurrencies, based on fundamental aspects of Bitcoin, have been created over the past couple of years. The first and greatest of the altcoins is Litecoin which was created in 2011 to address some flaws that may be in the Bitcoin protocol.

Litecoin is harder to build specialised mining machines for, which--according to its founders--prevents it from being dominated by a few rich miners. It also clears payments faster, and has a much higher cap of 84 mio coins.

| WOW, VERY CRYPTOCURRENCY |

Litecoin seems to have been eclipsed by another altcoin with a far more compelling hook: Dogecoin.

Dogecoin is a triumph of marketing. Take a field anyone can enter, where the average user has little or no way to distinguish between competing examples and create a meme that involves pictures of a confused-looking Shiba Inu, make it a brightly coloured comic with text surrounding it, spelling out, in broken English, the animal's thoughts. Wow.

It's a joke, of course, to appeal to the sort of person who would find it funny. And it worked—the total value of all Dogecoins in circulation is, as I write, worth almost $1 billion, making it the 36th most valuable alt coin in existence.

It seemed like Dogecoin was the pinnacle of the altcoin madness, but then came the news some coders were preparing to launch a cryptocurrency based on Kanye West, called, naturally, Coinye West, proving that the idea still has legs.

| Finally, my own Cryptocurrency |

Through the book, you got to know some of the cryptocurrencies, but there are still many, many more on the market. The reason for this is that all cryptocurrencies, starting from Bitcoin, are an open source software, and its codes are available on github.com. But not all IT people can manage to create a good quality clone, or fork off a cryptocurrency.

If you have an idea or a good concept, then it can make sense for you to launch your own cryptocurrency with a possible ICO. Doing this you can even acquire funds to start your project or business. All you need is a good idea for the project or business, and a team to support it.

Together, with my specialized Crypto IT team, we are helping regular people, with little or no knowledge, to create Crypto-related software for their needs: creation of the new cryptocurrency, infrastructure around the coin, tools for the new or existing coins, marketing and performing your ICO.

So, everything is possible. Just dream it and dare to realize it.

For more information, contact Deki, at cryptocurrenciesbook@gmail.com

| Notes |

| Notes |

CHAPTER 13
WHY SHOULD I
INVEST IN AN ICO?

| **Chapter 13 -** Why Should I Invest in an ICO? |

An initial coin offering, or ICO, is an alternative form of crowdfunding used to start new cryptocurrency ventures. ICOs are used by start-ups since they are unregulated and allow them to bypass the rigorous and regulated capital-raising process required by venture capitalists or banks. This model has been very successful and has helped a lot of products and companies get the funding required to start their business.

The idea behind an ICO is to presale coins of a cryptocurrency, or tokens of a blockchain project, in exchange for established cryptocurrencies, like Bitcoin or Ethereum. It is a similar idea to the concept of an initial public offering (IPO): both are a process that companies use to raise capital. Since 2013, a common use of ICOs has been to fund the development of new cryptocurrencies. If there is demand for the pre-created token, it can easily be sold and traded on all cryptocurrency exchanges. Some project that after the Ethereum ICO, and other successful ICOs, the concept could become a tool that may revolutionize the whole financial system. If ICOs continue this path, the ICO token could become the securities and shares of the future.

Tokens issued from an ICO can have a value because the ICO allocates the equivalent to equity to the token. This gives the investors in the ICO ownership voting rights and, in certain cases, qualifies them for dividends. It is this form of ICO that is closest in nature to IPOs.

However, the vast majority of ICOs issue tokens that are an asset, which gives investors access to the feature of a particular project rather than ownership of the company itself. Ultimately, this is the process of crowdfunding a new cryptocurrency project. This involves a token sale, with the cryptocurrency project raising capital to fund operations; in return, the investors receive an allocation of the project's tokens.

ICOs are usually open for period of a few weeks to a month. Sometimes, though, they can be open for longer, and unlike an IPO, which is a one-time EVT, it is possible for an ICO to take place on multiple occasions.

| How Does ICO Work, and How Do You Use ICO? |

When a start-up first plans an ICO, they kick-start the process by establishing the blockchain and setting up protocols and rules. After this point, an ICO date is announced.

The next step for the creator is to begin mining for coins that will be sold during the ICO. Most also use social media sites and a rising number of cryptocurrency related websites as a marketing medium with which to attract investors ahead of the ICO date. It's important for creators to draw in as much interest as possible, to not only raise the required funding for a successful ICO, but also to push demand and prices post ICO.

You can look up active and upcoming ICOs through various sites. The purchase of their cryptocurrencies can be made through the selected exchange, and investors may also be able to buy directly though the creator's official website. The documentation requirements for investing in ICOs vary, depending upon the investor's country of residence. The requirements should be outlined on the respective exchange's site, and creator's website.

| A step-by-step of an ICO can be summarized as follows: |

The first step of an ICO is the pre-announcement, which acts as the marketing stage of the future project. The creators market these through sites frequented by cryptocurrency investors. During this process, the creators of the project will prepare the white paper. The white paper is essentially an investor presentation, where the creators outline the details of the project.

After the white paper has been circulated, the company will listen to investors to see if the proposed project has a good level of interest. After getting a sense of the interest, the company will then address concerns and risks of would-be investors, before reaching a final business model and final version of the white paper. The final version of this white paper is called the offering. It sets out the contract's terms for the benefit of the investor and is made on behalf of the company that is entering into the ICO.

The offer contains several pieces of important information. It will outline the project details, the total amount of capital required, as well as the project timelines. It will also indicate which financial instrument will be sold during the ICO—this is usually tokens. Whatever the financial instrument is, it will have a value assigned to it, along with the rights of the investors, and the expected period after which the company will commence returning earnings to investors. These earnings are traditionally dispensed via dividends. The ICO start date is announced after this offer has been signed. From then, until the start date, the marketing campaign moves into overdrive.

The marketing campaign is a pivotal component of an ICO. It serves such an important role because it is what drives the interest that is required to raise the necessary capital. Since companies planning ICOs are often nascent and unknown, they usually need to hire marketing agencies to help make the necessary presentation, etc. Campaigns, on average, last a month, and target institutions and some smaller investors as their audience. When using a crowdfunding program, the individual participants are usually the main segment of focus as investors and are more willing to back projects when their involvement in the project is positive for both the investor and the company.

Following the end of marketing, the buying and selling of tokens commences, with the company having established an exchange for investors to acquire tokens

For more detailed information, contact Deki at cryptocurrenciesbook@gmail.com

| Notes |

| Notes |

CHAPTER 14
PROS AND CONS REGARDING ICOs

| Chapter 14 - Pros and Cons Regarding ICOs |

| For companies raising capital through ICOs, the advantages include: |

- In contrast to companies that fundraise via IPOs, the project is not necessarily subject to direct taxation.

- Sales of coins or tokens are direct and have few, if any, required intermediaries throughout the process, and investors base their investment decisions on the content of white papers prepared by the fundraising entity.

- This process can have multiple rounds.

| For Investors in ICO |

Regulation: There have been advancements in the cryptocurrency regulatory landscape; countries, such as Japan and Russia, have now recognized cryptocurrencies as legal tender. However, ICOs have yet to fall under the cloak of regulators.

Recently, in the US, the SEC announced that ICOs need to protect the investor. The size of the market has caught the government regulators' attention, and certain regulators and governments have now caught up on blockchains and the likes of Bitcoin and Ethereum. Regulators are responsible for even the most foolhardy of investors, and it's clear that some oversight could save a lot of pain for them, particularly as fraudulent cases begin to rise alongside the ever-increasing number of ICOs. The SEC has said that it will look into ICOs should they become a significant component of the market for investments, and a triggering event takes place, with companies looking to raise capital by way of ICOs becoming subject to both regulatory and enforcement action.

The lack of transparency with the US government remains an issue, and there have been reports that the sale of tokens to U.S citizens is in fact deemed illegal. Although whether exemptions will be permitted remains to be seen, the uncertainty is certainly there for investors to consider down the road.

One only has to look at current cryptocurrency valuations to understand why regulators would not sit on the sidelines. Since the total number of ICOs is rising, there is an inherent risk in investing in start-ups in this manner, and the fate of ICOs will be determined by how both investors and companies respond to the magnifying class of regulators. Regardless, since they remain able to raise sizable sums as a result of the large valuations of cryptocurrencies such as Bitcoin and Ethereum, it is an area all investors should consider.

It is certain that legal recourse to start-ups, with enforcement agencies that can take action against scammers and fraudsters, will be great additions, as less savvy investors are certainly there to be taken advantage of by the few who are so inclined.

| Should I Invest in ICO or Not? |

Many investors have been wowed by the recent returns and the surge in market cap of cryptocurrencies. While tremendous opportunities are certainly possible, and sound investment opportunities exist, there are also risks you need to consider before entering the blockchain world.

As is the case with all investments, and even more so where the investor has the possibility of returns in excess of a 100 percent, there are pros and cons that anyone investing must consider.

The Positives

- A large number of companies have raised enough capital through ICOs to become incredibly successful. This is despite the number of ICOs hitting the market, sometimes as many as a 100 every few weeks.

- Although, where returns are on the higher side, there is a higher level of risk associated with investing, the number of high ROI (Return on Investment) stories certainly provides an opportunity for those investors who are yield-hungry.

- In contrast to more traditional investment in start-ups where investor money can be tied in for years, the tokens from an ICO are considered liquid. Investors in an ICO can cash in and out at any point in the time that they would like, by converting ICO tokens into Bitcoin and other cryptocurrencies, as long as demand exists.

- Investors often face fees when dealing with IPOs, and VCs often like to run the show and make unnecessary demands, which, on occasion, devalue the investment. Due to this, companies can lose their identity in search of the dollar. With ICOs, these fees do not occur, and there aren't VC-like demands.

Some of the negative aspects concerning investing in an ICO include:

- ICOs are well-known for failures. Sometimes there are too many projects that are alike, and at other times, projects fail to reach expected levels. Both can drive the value of initial coins to zero.

- Since there is a lack of governance, it can be easy for investors, who haven't done their due diligence, to be deceived. This can leave naive investors open to Ponzi schemes and more.

- While ICOs have large possible upside, they are not ultimately something to bet your shirt on. Investments lost because of scams and frauds are unlikely to be recovered.

It is essential for investors to do a fair amount of due diligence because of the lack of regulatory oversight. This view has been repeated a lot; the number of fraudulent ICOs is likely to be on the rise as regulators lag behind this segment.

Due diligence tends to be an expensive process. For cryptocurrency economies and ICOs, the market has begun to see a rise in the presence of rating agencies. These agencies conduct due diligence and carry out the necessary analysis of the information at hand. The rating agencies then publish their research and, through this, reduce some of the risks associated with investing in ICOs. This type of self-policing comes ahead of any more formal regulatory oversight.

ICO Rating is an example of one of the agencies undertaking the task of providing some cover for investors and the analysis. This is certainly a good starting point to drive the ICO market to the next level. One must still be careful though—even rating agencies have been known to get it wrong occasionally.

In addition to the ratings, investors can also look out for ICOs that include independent escrow agents. This makes it so the capital raised does not reach the company entering an ICO, but instead, a 3rd party.

One example of such an escrow agent is Multi-Sig. In this example, an agent essentially funds a project on an ongoing basis, with funds released from an escrow as needed. The agent ensures that project targets are being met as measured by the company's pre-determined obligations to the investor.

While there is some level of control in entering the ICO market, some are wary this is another dot-com boom. Skeptics have been in force since the Global Financial Crisis, and almost every new investment opportunity has been labelled an economic bubble. This even included Bitcoin.

For now, however, ICO fund raising falls well short of the levels seen during the dot-com era. This should provide some level of comfort: the only concern in regards to a collapse in the market should be the volume of fraudsters, surge over the near-term, or that there is a collapse in the valuation of cryptocurrencies.

The association is ultimately coming off the back of the surge in valuations and market cap of the sector. It should be noted that this surge in market cap is not isolated to blockchains. Many start-ups hitting the market are looking to take advantage of the yield-hungry investor; thus, calling it a bubble, for now, is certainly just a more pessimistic view point. One needs only to look back at the early days of tech stocks, like Intel, Apple, Microsoft, and Alphabet, to realize how the industry can be reshaped in the years ahead.

The entrance of new sorts of regulatory oversight to ICO market should bring some form of longevity. Though the attractiveness of ICOs may be lost if the minimum requirements become too intensive, this kind of outcome would not kill off the industry but just change the medium through which capital is raised. As it stands, it is still pretty easy for creators right now.

For now, ICOs remain a phenomenon; but tomorrow, if companies and investors are not careful, it could be just another cautionary tale, joining the ranks of the dot-com, and stories of the recent pace. How ICOs continue to grow will boil down to the integrity of the sector and the success of companies raising capital. Investors have to be mindful that not all will deliver, but as long as the majority do, all should be fine.

| Notes |

| Notes |

CHAPTER 15

CHAPTER 15
CRYPTOCURRENCIES WITH ADDED VALUE

| **Chapter 15 -** Cryptocurrencies with Added Value |

The idea of adding value to cryptocurrencies is coming from the world we know. First, money or coins hold a real value. For example, the first coins were made from copper and, later, from gold and silver, and a mixture of both, which was called electrum, or other metals. These metals obviously held value in themselves, and one could easily measure them by weight. Physical coins were used a long, long time ago; for example, copper coins from 8th century BC have been found in China. Fiat money was also backed (not so long ago) with value in real gold—the so called gold standard. This means that if the central bank received new gold bars, then they had the right to print new money. But this is already in the past. There is no more gold standard in fiat currency—only printing new money without sustainability.

Because of this, some inventors in the cryptocurrency world imagined to make a gold standard for cryptocurrency. They have tried it in different ways. Some cryptocurrencies were supported by real material value—some by an idea. There are coins backed by precious materials, like stones, gold, diamonds, silver, etc. Furthermore, there are coins backed up with other commodities, like oil, gas, and electricity. People have even thought of backing coins with other cryptocurrencies, like Bitcoin.

This kind of action gives people a certain dose of trust because there is a possibility to exchange this cryptocurrency with the backed value, or preciousness, behind every unit of the coin. The only concern regarding this method is to trust the authors (the system) of the coin that they will really collect those assets for the coin and keep them secured and untouched. In most cases, they have proof of the assets, and can also demonstrate the possibility of taking out the assets if needed.

There have been many ICO based on coins with an idea supporting them rather than physical assets. Most of them are building a system to support their own community. For example, there was an ICO for the coin that supports the live music industry with the idea that musicians can be paid with this coin. All of them can also find gigs on their platform. So, they combined a platform where musicians can get a job and be paid in the supported currency, from the same platform. The idea was so good that it raised more than $12 million. And this is not the only case of a good idea. There are plenty of them on the Internet.

People might doubt the currencies they operate with. But the truth is that money's (currency's) value has been changing through time. And sometimes money (currency) even lost all the value on the market. Governments can make changes, and sometimes they can literally do it over night (like history is telling us). At the end is the trust that people have through holding and operating with money from the government. So, people show it still has value. If nobody would want it, it would be worthless and useless. The real value is when somebody is willing to give you something in exchange for the currency you are holding. It does not matter if it is a fiat or a crypto currency. Maybe now is the moment to rethink what a warranty is, and what it means to you! I believe there exists no guarantees. At the end, it is all about feelings and the psychology of the market.

Please contact Deki at cryptocurrenciesbook@gmail.com

| Notes |

CHAPTER 16
SECURITY IN THE CRYPTOCURRENCY WORLD

─────────

| **Chapter 16 -** Security in the Cryptocurrency World |

Most of us believe that security is crucial in the financial world. And I believe it too. Regardless of which matter is considered, even from the beginning of mankind, security/safety has most likely been a concern high ranked in people's minds. In the same way that prehistoric man stored and hid his meal from possible theft from other people or animals, the idea to securely store and hide digital assets is run by the same part of the brain. There are many ways a person can lose his/her valuable assets. For this reason, I want to give you some tips on what you have to be careful about, and how to avoid possible losses in the crypto world.

The first thing to think about is the storing of your cryptocurrency. This is one of the largest issues (in past years) concerning cryptocurrency losses. There are many stories out there about people who mined, bought, or received BTC in the early stages of cryptocurrency (long before the Crypto mania of today), only to lose their digital currency. The most powerful story is that of James in the U.K. In 2009, he had mined and stored, on his laptop hard drive, 7,500 BTC. At that time, it was very easy to mine BTC. In fact, he mined this amount with a single laptop. Then, his computer broke down, and he saved the hard drive disk. But one day, while cleaning, he found the hard drive in a drawer and threw it away. Yes, he threw away 7,500 BTC stored on the disk, with all the data on it! You can calculate on your own what he lost in today's value.

However, to be accurate, the mistake James made was not by throwing the disk away. His mistake was that he didn't save his wallet's private key. So, how do you avoid this kind of loss? The answer is simple: make a backup of your wallet or save your private key!

| What is a private key? |

A private key is a unique code formed by numbers and letters that represent a wallet balance in the cryptocurrency blockchain. There are many kinds of private keys.

A private key is a secret number allowing cryptocurrency to be spent by the holder of that key. Every cryptocurrency wallet contains one or more private keys, which are saved in the wallet.dat file. Private keys are mathematically related to any addresses generated for the wallet.

The private key is the ticket that allows someone to spend a cryptocurrency. Because of this, it is important that such keys are kept secure. Private keys can be kept on computer files, but in some cases, they are also short enough that they can be printed out on paper (a more secure version).

Some wallets allow private keys to be imported without generating any transactions. Other platforms will sweep a private key, which generates a transaction that sends the balance, controlled by that key, to a new wallet address. Just as with any other transaction, there is risk of swept transactions being double-spent.

In contrast, some cryptocurrencies provide a facility to import a private key without creating a sweep transaction. This is considered very dangerous and is not intended to be used, even by power users or experts, except in very specific cases. Bitcoins can be easily stolen, at any time, from a wallet that has imported an untrusted or otherwise insecure private key—this can include private keys generated offline and never seen by someone else.

Most of the wallets today are giving us an easier way to save the private key: in the form of a seed. Depending on the wallet, the seed can represent from 12 to 24 randomly generated English words and, when inserted in the right sequence, will sweep the balance of the private key to the desired wallet address.

So, the most important thing to do before you are using a wallet is to make a backup copy of your wallet. However, I believe that the printed, physical version of your private key is the most secure way to avoid having your cryptocurrency stolen online. Of course, you then have to take security measurements to store the physical version of your private key somewhere safe.

I strongly recommend you do the backup of your wallet alone, without anybody around you! And if you have the option of doing it offline, without an internet connection, it is even better and safer.

| Phishing |

Phishing in the crypto world is the most common form of abuse or fraud. There are fake websites that can fool you into thinking they are legitimate; and they can get the credentials of your account on the exchange platform or wallet provider. They can then take your balance by transferring it to another address. Once done, there is no possibility of getting your coins back. My advice: ALWAYS CHECK THE WEBPAGE URL OF THE WEBSITE ON WHICH YOU ARE ENTERING YOUR CREDENTIALS!!! This is the only way you can prevent giving your credentials to a crook.

One of the phishing methods I've come across is someone getting your credentials through email by pretending they were someone else. My advice again: DO NOT SHARE ANY CREDENTIALS OR SECURE INFORMATION THROUGH AN EMAIL. NO REAL PROVIDER SERVICE OR SUPPORT WILL ASK YOU FOR IT BY EMAIL; ONLY CROOKS WILL DO THIS!!!

If this happens on one of your wallet provider's accounts, contact their live support, and ask for immediate help. If the funds have not yet been processed in the transaction pool of the blockchain, then there is still time to stop those transactions. But once the transactions are in the pool, it is too late. Nobody can help anymore! Note: as security measures vary from platform to platform, try to choose one that has live support as an option. After all, you'll never know when you might need some help.

Similar to the last example, if your funds have been stolen from an account on the exchange platform, and they haven't yet transferred the funds to an external wallet address, there is a possibility that the exchange can block your account and make an investigation to see what happened. In this case, the funds may still be safe. But you need to discover the abuse at the earliest stage, and the helpline needs to respond immediately. In most cases, you'll be dealing with cunning crooks who know what they are doing. This means your funds can and will be in danger.

One of the cases I've heard about from a friend of mine was the cleverest way to abuse an exchange account that I've seen in my life. They didn't make any transaction to transfer his funds to another external wallet. But they bought, in abundance, a very cheap, as yet unknown, cryptocurrency on that exchange. When they acquired his credentials, they began to buy their sell orders of this cheap cryptocurrency at a very high price. This means that they bypassed all the security measures of the exchange—like email confirmation or a 2FA (second-factor authorization)—that is needed for an external transaction. In this case, they emptied his BTC account and left him with a bunch of worthless cryptocurrencies instead.

What I want to say with this example is that crooks are always in step with the times and are prepared to take away everything from unprepared people. Of course, exchanges are working on security improvements all the time. In fact, most of their business expenses come from the continuous development of their security systems!

But what can you do to prevent this?

- Change passwords frequently and use unique passwords for every account (not the same password that you have for your inbox, for example).
- Do not share your credentials with anybody online by using emails or social media chats.
- Always use the maximum level of security provided by the platform: email verification and 2FA.
- Only leave on the exchange the amount of currency with which you want to trade; use other safer possibilities to store your remaining coins.

I think the safest way to store your digital assets is still an offline wallet. With proper security measures and instructions, it can be the safest place to store your assets.

For more information regarding security in the crypto world, contact Dejan Deki Markovic at cryptocurrenciesbook@gmail.com

| Notes |

| Notes |

CHAPTER 17
PAPER AND OFFLINE WALLETS

| **Chapter 17 -** Paper and Offline Wallets |

Paper and offline wallets are both forms of cold storage. Cold storage is when you keep a reserve of cryptocurrency offline. This is often a necessary security precaution, especially when dealing with large amounts of cryptocurrency.

| **Methods of cold storage include keeping cryptocurrency:** |

- on a physical medium, such as paper.
- on a USB, or other data storage medium, in a safe place (e.g., safe deposit box, safe, etc.)
- in a professional hardware wallet service.

All of these cold storage methods have potential problems; but with proper care, they can be mitigated. I know of a number of cases where secret/private keys, and/or backup seeds, were lost because of where they were stored. The more common mediums of the above forms of cold storage are listed with some of their weaknesses.

| **Physical Mediums** |

These forms of mediums include paper (written or printed), laminated paper, and being engraved/etched/ ablated/stamped on a piece of metal. Proper paper wallets are a secure way of storing bitcoins because they aren't typically exposed to malware. They can also be stored in safes and safety deposit boxes. However, due to the current sub-optimal software support, it may be easier to make a mistake that causes loss of bitcoins.

Common Issues:

- The biggest issue in security is that anyone who can see it, can steal it.
- Human writing or printing errors can make things hard to read, or completely illegible.
- Human error in transcription can cause errors on the end product.
- Physical mediums are prone to damage (e.g., paper can rot, be torn, burn, or be smoke-damaged, while engraved metals can corrode).

Security Tips and Preventative Measures:

- Fireproof, or fire-resistant, boxes can help protect paper in a small house fire. It should be noted that they can sometimes fall apart in the fire or get wet when water is used to put out the fire. People can also just carry out a small, unsecured safe.
- The private seed proves your right to spend cryptocurrency that has been transferred to a paper wallet. As such, the private seed should be kept hidden and secret. If it's exposed (for example, in a photograph), then the wallet may be used by anyone who sees it.
- To guard against accidental revelation, the private key displayed on the paper wallet may be encrypted or split into several different parts.
- Disconnecting from the Internet is important because it guarantees that the paper wallet generator is truly self-contained and isn't transmitting your keys online.
- Some advanced printers have internal storage (even hard drives) that preserves copies of printouts. However, if someone gets access to your printer, or if you dispose of your printer, there's a possibility that the printer can be hacked.

Summary:

- Generating paper wallets is not recommended from an online PC. Malware on the PC can steal your wallet keys.
- Even if you generate paper wallets securely, they're still vulnerable to loss and theft.
- Unencrypted paper wallets must be kept just as safe as jewels or cash.
- One thing you can do to protect paper wallets is to split them into shares, requiring X of Y shares (e.g., 3 out of 5) to reassemble the secret key.

Digital Mediums

Common Issues:

- Computers crash and can make data recovery expensive.
- Data can still be recovered after a system is abandoned by the user. In some cases, data can be recovered after multiple overwriting attempts and physical destruction.
- Computers can burn or be smoke damaged.
- A traditional hard disc drive can have data corrupted by powerful magnetic fields, and can physically shatter.
- Magnetic media (tapes, floppy discs) can also be damaged by magnets.
- Rapidly changing magnetic fields (see MRIs) can damage the data stored on flash drives.
- A non-negligible amount of HDDs suffer from factory defects that will cause them to fail unexpectedly during their lifetime.
- Solid state drives (SSDs) can lose data if unpowered; they may last for years before this becomes a problem, but it's unwise to store long-term data in unpowered SSDs.
- If connected to the Internet, it is another attack vector, and the safety is only as good as the encryption used.
- If not connected to the Internet, safety is only as good as the physical protection encryption used: could someone break into the location, and copy the data without anyone noticing?

- Plastics break down over time, during exposure to heat, humidity, regular light, and all sorts of chemicals, even the oxygen in the air. This can lead to the loss of your data when stored on a medium made of plastic or written/printed on plastic.

Security Tips and Preventative Measures:

- External HDDs are good for storage for a few years at least, if stored properly.
- Make sure any computer used is clean and air-gapped (is a measure that ensures a secure computer network is isolated from unsecured networks).
- Your data can only be as safe as the security you have in place!

Professional Hardware Wallet Service:

A hardware wallet is a wallet that stores the user's private keys in a secure hardware device.

They have major advantages over standard software wallets:

- private keys are often stored in a protected area of a microcontroller and cannot be transferred out of the device in plaintext.
- they're immune to computer viruses.
- they can be used securely and interactively, unlike a paper wallet that must be imported to software at some point.
- the software is usually open source, allowing a user to validate the entire operation of the device.

Two of the major hardware wallet services are Trezor and Ledger, and there's a vault service provided by Xapo.

Trezor:

- Trezor is a hardware wallet that provides advanced security for handling cryptocurrency private keys.
- It is essentially a small computer that is designed to keep your private keys safe from possible online and offline risks.

- It is both secure bitcoin storage and a transaction signing tool.
- Due to its design, you can connect Trezor to an infected computer and still be able to have 100% control over the funds in your device.
- Private keys are generated by the device, and never leave it; thus, they cannot be accessed by malware.

Ledger:

- Ledger makes several cryptocurrency wallets.
- Ledger Wallet Nano S is a USB cryptocurrency wallet, which has smartcard security in a very compact package.
- Ledger Blue is available via pre-order and is an advanced hardware security device that boasts multiple application execution on a handheld device. It's designed around a secure element, and features a touchscreen, USB, and Bluetooth connectivity.
- Both offer similar security features to Trezor.

Xapo:

- Xapo is a company that provides a cryptocurrency wallet combined with a cold storage vault and a bitcoin-based debit card.
- Xapo uses offline encrypted servers.
- The servers are stored in vaults with restricted and monitored access.
- Their redundant, global network of storage vaults is designed to ensure no single security breach or regulatory action would ever compromise your account.

| Notes |

| Notes |

CHAPTER 18
EDUCATE YOURSELF AND USE THE KNOWLEDGE IN YOUR FAVOR

| Chapter 18 - Educate Yourself and Use the Knowledge in Your Favor |

We all know, at the end, it doesn't matter what we know; the only thing that counts is what we actually do. The world is changing, and new opportunities are constantly coming out. Maybe you recognize yourself as person who was observing some opportunities in the market, and later regretted not being involved in those opportunities. You aren't alone in this. Let me tell you one true story.

Some time ago, my mother and father-in-law came to me with the story of how they heard, on the radio, the news about the crazy growth of the bitcoin. This led them to think about buying some. But they only stood with the intent of doing it. They started to think about how it was cheap at the beginning, and how much they lost already by not buying it before. So, this intent of buying bitcoins went into oblivion. At that time, the price for a single unit was below $3,000. Then, after less than six months, Bitcoin, for the first time, broke the $20,000 milestone for a single unit. By the way, this represents more than 666% of profit. We met again in this period and talked again about the even more crazy growth. And you know what? They were again in the same loop of thinking, as at the beginning.

What can we learn from this example? That it hurts less if you tried and didn't succeed, than if you didn't try! Even surveys were made on the topic of doing and not doing things. They were asking elderly people what they regretted the most in their lives. And the results showed that they mostly regretted the things that they had never tried or done—not the mistakes they had made!

But I will give you one tip: Bitcoin is not alone in the market. There are plenty of cryptocurrencies out there. And like all things in life, nothing is warranted and 100% good. This means that many of them probably won't be successful in the future, while there will be some of them that shall assimilate in the future financial world.

When this book comes out, we will still be at the beginning. There are lots of countries where people still don't have a clue about what cryptocurrency is. In my opinion, it's the big investors, hedge funds, huge concerns, and so on, that are investing right now. Masses of people have yet to join this magnificent technological and financial world. There are plenty of different ways to participate in the crypto world. It is up to you to choose where you want to be included. So, TAKE ACTION! Now is the right time to use what you have learned from this book.

And remember, money will not bring you happiness; it's only a tool that can help you reach your goals (and that will make you happy). A successful person is a person who has success in different fields of life. Here are some to think about: familial, social, mental, physical, vocational, spiritual, and financial. But I will talk about this topic, on some other occasion.

I wish you a prosperous life, and abundance.

For more info regarding possible cooperation, contact Deki at cryptocurrenciesbook@gmail.com

| Notes |

GLOSSARY

2FA

Two-factor authentication is a solution that offers an additional layer of security. It keeps attackers who know the victim's password from passing an authentication check. It has been used for quite some time to control access to sensitive systems and data. Online services are increasingly introducing 2FA to prevent their user data from being accessed by hackers who have stolen a password database or have used phishing campaigns to obtain users' passwords.

Address

A Bitcoin address is like a physical address or an email. It's the only information you need to provide for someone to pay you with Bitcoin. An important difference, however, is that a different address should be used for each transaction.

Bit

Bit is a common unit designating a sub-unit of a bitcoin: 1,000,000 bits are equal to 1 bitcoin (BTC or ฿). The bit is usually more convenient for pricing tips, goods, and services.

Bitcoin

Bitcoin, with capitalization, is used when describing the concept of Bitcoin, or the entire network itself. (e.g., "I was learning about the Bitcoin protocol today.")

Without capitalization, bitcoin is used to describe bitcoins as a workunit of account (e.g., "I sent 10 bitcoins today."). It's often abbreviated as BTC or XBT.

Bitcoin Mining

Bitcoin mining is the process of having computers do mathematical calculations for the Bitcoin network, confirmirming transactions and increasinng security.

Bitcoin miners collect transaction fees for their work, along with newly created bitcoins. Mining is a specialized and competitive market, where the rewards are divided up according to how much calculation is done. Not all Bitcoin users do Bitcoin mining, and it is not an easy way to make money.

Block

A block is a record that contains and confirms many waiting Bitcoin transactions. Roughly every 10 minutes, a new block is appended to the existing chain of blocks of verified transactions (blockchain), through mining. Note: the current rate of mining determines that a block is worth 25 bitcoins.

Blockchain

The blockchain is a public record of Bitcoin transactions in chronological order. It establishes the permanence of Bitcoin transactions and prevents double spending.

BTC

BTC designates one bitcoin (฿).

Confirmation

Confirmation means that a particular transaction has been processed by the network and is highly unlikely to be reversed. Transactions receive a confirmation when they are included in a block in the blockchain. Even a single confirmation can be considered secure for low value transactions, although for larger amounts, like 1000 USD, you should wait for six confirmations or more. Each new confirmation decreases the likelihood of your transaction being reversed.

Cryptography

Online commerce and banking already uses cryptography, a branch of mathematics that allows us to formulate proofs that provide high levels of security. Bitcoin uses cryptography to make it impossible for anyone to spend funds from another user's wallet, or to corrupt the blockchain. Cryptography can also be used to encrypt a wallet, so that it can't be used without a password.

Double Spend

If a user tries to spend their bitcoins with two different recipients at the same time, this is referred to as double spending. Bitcoin mining and the blockchain prevent double spending by creating a consensus regarding which of the transactions will be confirmed and considered valid.

Ethereum

Ethereum wants to be a world computer that would decentralize—and some would argue, democratize—the existing client-server model.

With Ethereum, servers and clouds are replaced by thousands of so-called nodes (computers), run by volunteers across the globe (forming a world computer).

Ethereum intends to use this super computer to allow people anywhere in the world to offer services on top of this infnrastructure.

Apps and online services now rely on the company (or another third-party service) to store your credit card information, purchasing history, and other personal data somewhere, generally in servers controlled by third-parties.

In the instance of an online document service like Evernote or Google Docs, Ethereum plans to turn control of the data in these types of services over to its owner, and the creative rights to its author.

The idea is that no single entity will have control over your notes, and that no one could suddenly ban the app itself, temporarily taking all of your notebooks offline. Only the user can make changes—not any other entity.

In theory, it combines the control that people had over their information in the past, with the easy-to-access information that we're used to in the digital age. Each time you save edits, or add or delete notes, every node on the network makes the change.

Everledger

Everledger is a blockchain-based fraud-detection system for valuable physical assets like jewelry and diamonds. It combines the bitcoin blockchain with its own blockchain to build smart contracts that certify diamonds, jewelry, etcetera. It combats the sale of conflicting products (like blood diamonds) by keeping a transaction history for each item.

Fork

A fork is a situation where a blockchain splits into two separate chains. Forks generally happen in the crypto-world when new governance rules are built into the blockchain's code.

It is also used for a clone of an existing cryptocurrency.

Hash Rate

The hash rate is the measuring unit of the processing power of the Bitcoin network. The Bitcoin network must make intensive mathematical operations for security purposes. Example: when the network reached a hash rate of 10 Th/s, it meant it could make 10 trillion calculations per second.

Private Key

A private key is a piece of secret data that proves your right to spend bitcoins from a specific wallet using a cryptographic signature. Your private key(s) are stored in your computer if you use a software wallet; they are stored on some remote servers if you use a web wallet. Private keys must never be revealed, as they allow you to spend bitcoins from their respective Bitcoin wallet.

A cryptographic signature is a mathematical construct that allows someone to prove ownership ocertain bitcoins. In the case of Bitcoin, a wallet and its private key(s) are linked by mathematical magic. When your Bitcoin software signs a transaction with the appropriate private key, everyone on the network has the ability to see that the signature matches the bitcoins being spent. However, there's no way for the world to know your private key and to steal your hard-earned bitcoins.

PTP

Peer-to-peer is a system that allows each individual to interact directly with others. In the case of Bitcoin, the network is built in such a way that each user is broadcasting the transactions of other users. And, crucially, no bank is required as a third party.

Smart Contracts

In the context of blockchains and cryptocurrencies, smart contracts are pre-written logic (computer code), stored and replicated on a distributed storage platform (e,g,. a blockchain). These contracts are executed/run by a network of computers (usually the same ones running the blockchain). they can result in ledger updates like cryptocurrency payments, etcetera.

In other words, they are tiny programs that say "if this happens, then do that," and are run and verified by many computers to ensure trustworthiness.

If blockchains give us distributed trustworthy storage, then smart contracts give us distributed trustworthy calculations.

For further information on this topic, contact Dejan Deki Markovic at cryptocurrenciesbook@gmail.com

Wallet

A Bitcoin wallet is loosely the equivalent of a physical wallet, on the Bitcoin network. The wallet actually contains your private key(s), which allow you to spend the bitcoins allocated to it in the blockchain. Each Bitcoin wallet shows you the balance of all bitcoins it controls, and lets you use a specific amount to pay a specific person, just like a real wallet. This is different compared to credit cards, where you are charged by the merchant for the use of your card.

| Notes |

www.ingramcontent.com/pod-product-compliance
Lightning Source LLC
Chambersburg PA
CBHW062019200326
41519CB00017B/4849